A Year in my Garden

A Year in my Garden

Christine Buxton

A YEAR IN MY GARDEN

Design by Thalamus Publishing
4 Attorney's Walk, Bull Ring, LUDLOW, Shropshire SY8 1AA

Printed and bound in China

ISBN 10-digit: 1-902886-17-8
ISBN 13-digit: 978-1-902886-17-6

10 9 8 7 6 5 4 3 2 1
This book is printed on acid-free paper

Photographs by the author

CONTENTS

~ *Preface* ~

My mother-in-law, suffering from Motor Neurone Disease, and my father-in-law, realising he needed help to look after her, had been living with us for some time. The garden had been neglected, but still gave pleasure in the rare times we could take the wheelchair around it and the many times we could look out at it from the house, every window looking onto the garden or onto the lovely Corvedale. One of the reasons my parents-in-law decided to live with us was the wonderful views of the dale. When one is sick in body, one needs to be uplifted in spirit and our views certainly do that.

And then last month my mother-in-law died and suddenly we have time to fill and nothing to fill it with. So my garden has come to the rescue. I can begin to plan, to look forward with something other than dread and to enjoy the satisfaction that comes from being totally absorbed in a special project.

For Frank

INTRODUCTION ~ *The House and Garden*

Looking down on cloud
hanging low in the valley.

THIS BOOK AND THE GARDEN YEAR begin for me in May. Spring is here, the daffodils are going over and the lawn needs mowing once a week now. The lawn is the big project at the moment. Last year my husband Simon and I decided to improve the garden for wheelchair access, which meant moving the septic tank from the middle of the lawn and filling the gaping hole it left behind. So now we have to reseed. But first, a description of the house and garden.

We live in a hamlet in Shropshire at 850ft (259m) above sea level. We are at the highest point in the area and so have fine views of the Corvedale and of Titterstone Clee. Because we are fairly high here, in gardening terms we are about three weeks later than the nearest town, Ludlow, which, at 285ft (87m) is 565ft lower. This means that although we have to wait a little longer for the first flowers, they still look good when many others are past their best.

Shropshire is terribly popular at the moment for its beautiful countryside and lack of motorways, its characterful market towns and quaint villages, which makes it difficult to find a house for

Clee Hill viewed from our garden.

Shropshire's beautiful countryside: Angel Bank and Corvedale viewed from the highest point of Clee Hill. Our house sits towards the left of the long, cloud-shaded ridge, with sunlit Corvedale beyond. The town of Ludlow is just off the photograph's left edge.

sale which has a large garden. Queues of cash buyers are waiting to pounce the moment a garden comes on the market. We too fell in love with the peace and quiet of the Border country, but were pipped at the post so many times that we were forced to rent a house here to be ready to hand the cash over the instant an opportunity presented itself.

When the moment finally did arrive, we bought a lovely old cottage with two acres of land, a garden of one acre around the house and the other acre a rough paddock, where a neighbour's sheep graze and where we have our bonfires. I had always wanted a house with a large garden, or should I say 'a large garden with a nice house'. Our previous gardens were at most a third of an acre and I had always felt frustrated not being able to do anything on a grand scale. We are tucked away at the end of a quiet lane, our nearest neighbour a field away. On one side of the garden is a

Opposite: We always relax when we turn into the lane.

Beyond the fence a bridleway flanks fields where sheep graze.

field where sheep graze, giving us the pastoral idyll so many dream about. However, the dream is not all it's cracked up to be when little lambs are lost at five o'clock in the morning, bleating loudly for their mothers. That or the dawn chorus wakes us up. But we love it. On the other side of the garden is a lane, a bridleway, with a scrubby field alongside. More fields of sheep fall away into the valley and we have far-reaching views of the traditional, irregular patchwork of fields and woods.

We were faced with a garden that was mostly a field, apart from a few select horrors. There was a pink and white flagged terrace and a long, winding gravel path laid on concrete. This led from the garage through the lawn to a stagnant, plastic, two-tier pool with feature plastic heron. There were also three huge larch trees close to the house growing on top of the main drainpipe.

The ineffective disguise of sanitary fixtures had to go: a line of over-tall larch trees above the main drain and, at extreme left, a makeshift rockery hiding the property's septic tank.

And the septic tank had been cunningly disguised by turning it into a rockery of sorts – actually, by covering it in grey scalpings, adding a few rocks, a few plants in pots and a rickety, wooden wishing well. It took a great deal of time and money to get rid of these 'features', in fact almost a year, but then we had a clean slate, slightly daunting but hugely exciting. At last, I had the garden I had dreamt of!

The soil here, I discovered, is heavy clay, so for the most part we have no problems; everything grows extremely well and very few plants fail. It is always my fault if they do fail, for planting without checking the plants' cultural requirements. But everybody suffers from impulse buys, no matter how hard we try to harden our hearts to the temptations offered by a visit to a garden centre. However, heavy clay such as ours can be difficult to work, hard as rock in a dry summer and marshy in winter. And so each year I add a ton or two of sand to the flowerbeds to lighten the soil. The owner of a local nursery advised me to use cheap builders' sand rather than washed horticultural sand, as the ground can take it. This is a tip I am most grateful for as the builders' sand is only about £14 a ton. I also add as much compost, manure and lambs' litter as I can find and slowly the soil is becoming dark, friable and a pleasure to work. The first year we were here there was a very dry spell and though most plants survived, the clay was like concrete and could not be dug at all. I discovered that clay soils only retain 20 per cent water, whereas humus acts like a sponge and holds up to 80 per cent water. So now my mission is to make as much compost as I can, to turn my clay into loam.

Our house is an old stone-built cottage dating from around 1840, which has been added to over the years in both brick and stone. It was a long, low house originally, two up, two down with an adjoining stable and cowshed. When the cowshed end was converted into a sitting room and bedroom, the height of the house remained unchanged and so all the bedrooms are in the roof. This gives the bedrooms character, with sloping ceilings and nooks and crannies. We added an extension at one end of the

house for my parents-in-law, so now we have a very long, low cottage that from a distance looks like a row of terraced houses.

The garden has been planned to be in proportion with the low height of the roof. The first thing we did when we arrived was lay a terrace. But what size? After several fruitless visits to the library and scanning tedious books about construction, I finally found what I needed to know in a book by Rosemary Verey. The depth of the terrace should equal the height of the eaves. That seemed very deep to us at first, but once it was laid we found it perfect. However, I now think that it could have been even deeper, as when plants alongside grow over the edges, two or three feet of terrace are immediately lost. If I had thought of this, I would have allowed extra depth to compensate.

There is no longer any sign of the old cowshed, which was converted into a sitting room. The rambling rose on the wall helps the brick face to blend with the older stone.

The next task was to dig the flowerbeds and surround them by a yew hedge with plants barely a foot high. Again I tried to get the proportions correct relative to the height of the house and the depth of the terrace. I allowed a three-foot width for the hedge and a seven-foot depth for the flowerbeds. When the tiny yews were first planted, the flowerbeds looked enormous in comparison. But a couple of years on, I find I will have to increase the depth of the flowerbeds, as the yews, still only about three feet high, are beginning to overshadow the beds.

We then laid out an area for the vegetable garden next to the terrace and bordering the lane. Though it took us three years to finish the paths, we were able to grow vegetables right from the start. The shape is a long wedge with only one right angle. To make the space appear symmetrical I planted a holly, which I had growing in a pot for ten years, opposite the gate and at the far end of the site. When you enter the vegetable plot, your eye is drawn to the holly at the end and the odd shape of the site is not

The bare outline of the beds can be seen in winter. We used gravel and wood chip paths to divide the vegetable plot into several beds.

obvious. I wanted lots of small beds and paths to make maintenance easier, so the site was first divided into three with paths of stone and gravel. One third is for permanent plants such as gooseberries, strawberries, raspberries and asparagus. This decorative section has eight small beds with brick paths between them. The other two thirds, with six and eight beds, are for the usual crop rotation. The paths here are wood chippings, as we could not afford any more brick at the time. We put a gate at each end and put the compost bins outside the plot, just beyond the far gate. We took great pains to protect the vegetables from vermin. We are plagued by voracious rabbits, which sit

The trellis hides a gas tank in the cottage garden.

nonchalantly on the lawns and flowerbeds, blatantly eating the campanulas and any other rare and expensive plants they take a fancy to. They excavate burrows in the herbaceous borders and dig up the roots of the poor, struggling yew hedge. So we put wire netting around the vegetable garden, one foot underground and three feet above. Even though the rabbits enjoy the rest of the garden, the pleasures of the vegetable patch are unknown to them.

Then two years ago I made a tiny cottage garden next to the kitchen, where the washing line and gas tank are. There was a small, scruffy lawn there before, but now there are higgledy-piggledy stone paths and cottagey flowers all crammed in together. I planned this to be a spring garden, but because of self-seeding and impulse buys it looks pretty until October, when it reverts to green hummocks and calm.

Last year we built an arbour at the far end of the garden near the paddock, within a circle of shrubs which had been saved from the site of the new garage. We did this so that my mother-in-law

could have somewhere new to drive her wheelchair. The position was dictated by the view from the arbour to the hills 40 miles distant. We planted seven fruit trees to go with an existing damson to make a small alley leading to the arbour, with four trees on either side. This part of the garden is the most immature, but we hope to have a sheltered, private, secret spot there before long.

A quiet spot for reflection.

And finally, this year's project is to make a new lawn where the septic tank used to be. Beyond the smart lawn and flowerbeds was an expanse of turf with cesspit pipes and hatches poking up in the middle looking dreadful. That part of the garden had always been an eyesore, but I could never decide what to do with it. This ugly feature could be seen from everywhere, even from the kitchen looking down towards the paddock. Whenever anyone visited the garden they would ask, 'What are you going to do about the septic tank?' and then proceed to tell me what they thought I should do: plant shrubs around to hide it, put a summerhouse on top of it, make it into a rockery – all suggestions were duly considered. But I like the space; I like the view from the kitchen all the way down to the paddock and would not like it to be blocked by a gazebo or shrubs. Although the garden does feel a little too open at the moment, when the yew hedge around the flowerbeds grows, there will be plenty of enclosure and structure close to the house. The area nearer the paddock needed a less formal feeling. Besides, that area is large enough for a marquee if we have a party and for ball games when our family visits.

And so, last autumn the septic tank was moved, at great expense and with much grumbling from Simon, beyond the hedge to a corner of the paddock and we decided to keep a large lawn there and improve it. This 'septic tank' lawn had always sloped badly down to the lane and needed to be built up. So, when we were building a new garage, we saved the 30 tons of soil dug up from the foundations to use for levelling the ground. As usual, something went wrong with the timing. The chap who was to move the soil was ill in hospital and we have had a couple of months' delay. We have had to find someone else to bring the soil in and level it. So a job that should have been done in January is now being done in May. But I am ever hopeful that the grass will grow, even if the seed is sown rather late in May, as I would like to have a party on the lawn in July.

So at last, the basic layout of the garden is finished after six years. All that remains now is to enjoy it all while watching it grow.

MAY ~ *Snakes, Hedgehogs and Other Exciting Events*

Previous page:
Work in progress
on the new lawn.

THIS MORNING I TOOK the first photo for the new, gardening year, an uninspiring mound of soil and the second photo, the ugly gash in the lawn where the septic tank used to be. Today is the big day. After three years of trying to decide what to do with the area beyond the flower beds, we are very close to removing the last traces of the old cesspit. The digger and dumper are both here and the men are moving the mound of soil stored in the paddock to the garden, and roughly levelling it for rotavating next weekend. Having been delayed for a couple of months, we really need to get on quickly with seeding the lawn.

The weather is not good, wetter than I had liked and with clay soil there is a danger of the lawn settling later into hollows and bumps. But we need to do it now for that day in summer when we will be relaxing in the sun, drinks in hand, admiring the beautiful, new lawn. I will congratulate myself on my foresight and brilliant design skills and smile modestly as the compliments come pouring in. Well, that is the general idea. But I may be bemoaning the lack of time to weed the area more thoroughly and remove all the loose stones before scattering the seed. I might also wish we had rolled the lawn instead of doing the 'gardeners' shuffle'. Preparation being the key, I might also regret not fertilising the soil, assuming as I do that clay has sufficient nutrients. But we will not know whether we have done enough until July, when we need to use the lawn. And by then it may be too late. I console myself in advance – we did our best, the weather was against us, that part of the garden is utilitarian turf not fine sward. Does this sound familiar? Will we ever be photographed for *Gardeners' World*? I do not believe so.

Next day. I was woken up at 6.45 by the noise of a digger. In my sleepy state I thought our landscapers had arrived and it must be 8.30 already. But then I noticed the time. When I opened the blind I found the garden bereft of soil-moving equipment. I ran to the back window and saw the chap from the equipment hire shop about to drive the digger up onto his transporter and take it away. The dumper was already on there. I bravely dashed across the drive in my dressing gown to rescue the digger! The soil-moving men were due in an hour and they were expecting to be able to use the digger. To save us money with the equipment, my landscapers had asked for the dumper to be taken off hire last night, as they reckoned they could manage with only the digger today. However, the office assistant had misunderstood and had taken both machines off hire and they were about to be abducted. Needless to say, I saved them!

If the new lawn is not quite ready for July, it will certainly need to be ready soon after, as a friend who works for a charity for the disabled has just asked me if I would allow a small group of disabled people to visit my garden in August. The visitors all live in towns and because of mobility or other difficulties would rarely visit a hamlet like ours. As I mentioned, we live at the end of a pretty lane, there are many stunning views in this area and the village has the feel of being off the beaten track. Visitors are always delighted by the neighbouring field of sheep and at the feeling of being in the country, even though they are so close to

So close are the sheep in the neighbouring field, they seem almost a part of our garden.

home. I jumped at the chance. I adore showing the garden to anybody and everybody. I love describing the plants, talking about future plans, asking for ideas. And this has given me an incentive to do a little more work and make more of an effort. It would be wonderful to say I need no motivation other than a passion for gardening, but truth be told, I always make more effort if there is an exam at the end, or in this case, visitors to impress.

Opposite: Weeded and mulched and showing new growth.

The weather has been against me this week. We sometimes have storms and floods in May, but this year has not been too bad with just light rain. However, the ground has been too wet to rotavate until today. I checked the state of the soil this afternoon, saw that the ground was nice and firm and rang the hire shop for a rotavator for tomorrow. Luckily, they had one available at such short notice, so I booked it for the weekend. Unluckily, two hours later it rained and the clay became unworkable. I suppose I should have checked the weather forecast; one lives and learns. This now means we will not be able to start work on the lawn until June, as I am busy every weekend from now until the end of May. The work must be done at weekends as my helpers are only available on Saturdays and I cannot do such heavy work alone. I do not mind too much, as there are so many other projects to get on with.

The ongoing work at the moment is weeding. I weed the beds, put the leaf mould down and then spread compost on top of it. It is good to do this now as the soil is still moist from the April showers and the mulch will retain the moisture until at least July. I have large amounts of leaf mould as I make my own. Every year I put autumn leaves from the mature oaks and sycamores that border our garden into plastic bin liners and put them in my nifty leaf mould bin – four posts with wire netting around. I make sure the leaves are moist and poke several holes in the bags to allow worms to get in. But every year the leaves decay at different rates. Some of the leaves rot down to a fine cake-mix-like substance, while others are still very obviously piles

26

Compost bins I
had made for £10
plus the wood.

of mushy leaves. However, this makes no difference at all to me, as I always put a layer of compost on top. Then the worms do all the work pulling the leaf mould into the soil and I have an empty bin ready for the next autumn – very satisfying.

Pretty but scary.

As I was shovelling compost out of the bin this week, I came across something rather exciting. I found ten snake's eggs buried a couple of feet down. I knew there had been snakes there, as last year when we were forking some grass clippings into the heap, we disturbed an enormous, terrifyingly scary snake. We ran for the camera, of course, and very, very carefully photographed it. It turned out to be a grass snake and perfectly harmless. It was several feet long and gave us all quite a fright. Grass snakes enjoy water, where they swim and hunt and as there is a small pond in the field next to our garden, I imagine we are on their territory. They also like rough habitats with long grass, so maybe their winter burrow is in our paddock. I hope it is. They lay their eggs in warm, rotting vegetation, so compost heaps are ideal. The eggs are a little bigger than a large hen's egg and creamy white. They must be fairly tough to withstand the weight of compost pressing down on them, yet they did not feel too leathery. I accidentally smashed three with my fork as I was digging and the stench was unbelievably nauseating, quite the worst I have ever smelled. A couple of the eggs had a tiny hole at one end and were empty; I assume some small creature with a very strong stomach had eaten those. I re-buried two eggs in the adjoining compost bin. It is doubtful that they will hatch but I live in hope.

There was another exciting event this week. Today we adopted a hedgehog! A few months ago my mother-in-law and I read an article about the Hedgehog Preservation Society in a gardening magazine (where else?). The article explained that one could adopt a blind or lame hedgehog. I thought this was a good idea for my mother-in-law, as she was passionate about wildlife and would be enormously interested in the goings-on of a little hedgehog. We thought that our vegetable plot would be an ideal habitat, as the whole plot is enclosed by rabbit-proof wire netting. This would ensure an undisturbed, safe home for the hedgehog. So I immediately rang the Hedgehog Preservation Society and offered to take a couple. However, as hedgehogs hibernate in winter, we have had to wait until spring for them and unfortunately, Madeline, my mother-in-law, has not lived to see them.

In our case, there were no disabled hedgehogs available and instead we have been given a mature male hedgehog with the promise of two younger females in a few weeks when they are a

William's house, with detached dining room.

little larger. Our hedgehog, which my father-in-law has named William for some reason (probably some literary reference of which I am sadly ignorant) has been in captivity for a year and needs to be released into the wild if possible. So we will keep him for six to eight weeks and then try to release him together with the females, which will have arrived by then. The preservation society people gave us a smart, wooden house and some food, namely a large tin of dog meat and some cat biscuits. I had already bought a bag of special food for William, rather disgusting squashed insects and suchlike. We must also put a dish of water out every day. I thought that hedgehogs eat barrowloads of slugs, which of course would be perfect in the vegetable garden, but according to my hedgehog book, slugs make up only three per cent of their diet. Apparently, three quarters of their food is beetles (nice and crunchy), caterpillars (good from my point of view) and earthworms (not so good for me). The remaining quarter consists of birds' eggs and various insects. Nevertheless, I am sure William will be an invaluable helper for us and we will not have any insect pests in the garden at all.

A third exciting thing this month is the purchase of a new lawnmower. It is a petrol-driven Honda with a left-handed pull-cord. Although I am practically ambidextrous, I find right-handed starters too difficult. I looked at key-ignition machines but they were too expensive, so the shop brought two different pull-cord mowers to my garden for a 'test-mow'. It was obvious which was the better mower for me in the test-drive, as one of them almost had to be pushed and was difficult for me to turn. If I had not been able to test the mowers at home I am sure I would have bought the wrong one. We tested them on the lawn and then on the long grass in the paddock. I wanted the new mower mainly for the paddock, as we had decided that we needed to make short-mown paths through it to use the area more often. I am delighted with the new mower and have now mown several paths through the long grass to the gate, the woodshed, around the bonfire etc. I love having a new toy.

Another of my gardening expenses this month is gravel for the drive. When we made the drive wheelchair-friendly by putting a level, stone path around the house, we did not have enough gravel to cover the edges of the new path, so we borrowed some from the drive and now need to top up those sparse areas. I have been too busy up to now to order more. A large drive is an absolute necessity for me. Not because I cannot manoeuvre the car, as some have unkindly suggested, but because we have so many visitors, both for us and for my father-in-law,

When the grass grows long later in the year, the mown paths stand in relief.

Tom. There are also gas tankers, oil tankers and various delivery vehicles, which can be enormous. Once, we had a bed delivered in a pantechnicon that was so high it broke several branches off the trees in the lane and almost did not make it to the house. As the lane proper ends at our gate and changes into a muddy bridleway with no vehicular access, we need somewhere for lorries to turn to go back down the lane. The space for a large drive is a Godsend. When we bought the house there was a huge, circular rockery in the middle of the drive for some reason. It made manoeuvring difficult and was completely weed infested. We planted it with lavender, which was very successful, but as

31

soon as we could afford to, we had it removed.

Choosing the gravel for the drive was tricky because the house has both grey-green stone and reddish brick. The local grey gravel which was already there looked very stark against the red brick and did not harmonise with the stone. So I chose a brown-beige mix from a local quarry, which imports the gravel from Derbyshire. This is much better with the disparate colours

Above left: Some of the shrubs around the drive, and left: the Derbyshire gravel with the stone terrace and wood chip on the new bed.

of the house and is a lovely, tawny brown when it rains; the only problem was the price – £98 per ton!

So I waited until Simon was out of the way on a business trip in Paris and then ordered two tons of gravel. His expression when I told him how much it had cost was indescribable. I stressed that I had saved money by ordering two tons for only £144, as quantity is always cheaper, but he did not seem to appreciate the cost effectiveness. Nevertheless, he does like the smart, finished drive.

This week I decided on a cosmetic improvement for the new

The avenue of fruit trees – apples, plums and damsons.

rows of fruit trees leading to the arbour. When they were planted I thought they would look pretty underplanted with daffodils. They do, but only for a few weeks. Now, in May, the daffodils' dying leaves in the long grass look incredibly messy for a month to six weeks, until they can be cut back. As this is a well-used walkway, the irritation of the untidy leaves outweighs the pleasure of the earlier blooms, so I have decided to mow over the daffodils and keep this area more formal. We have other areas where narcissi are planted en-masse, where they can be left to die in long grass and look quite pretty and cottagey. These are at the edges of the garden, further from the more formal planting near the house and closer to the neighbouring fields and hedges.

Garden Pests or 'The Perils of Living Near Sheep'

Last night we were watching television with one eye and watching two large rams pushing against the gate to the field with the other. We were idly speculating whether they might push the gate over, when they did just that. We ran out immediately, Simon by the back door and I by the front. You always have to have a two-pronged attack with sheep or they run off in the wrong direction. Three enormous (as they seemed to me) rams were in the garden and one of them looked as if he was here to stay. Thankfully, however, they decided to leave when Simon cunningly threatened them with mint sauce. And then we blocked the gap with two garden benches and lots of rope.

Lovely in the paddock, but a disaster in the garden.

I remember one morning last year when a whole flock came into the garden through the gate on the lane and I single-handedly shooed them out again. I was so proud of myself. But on another occasion we tried to get just three sheep back into the field from the lane and they eluded us and ended up a mile away. The local farmer searched for them for a couple of hours that day.

Sheep do get into the garden once or twice a year, but luckily

have always been spotted before they could do any damage. We are not so lucky with my father-in-law's springer spaniel, Bess. Since coming here she has started digging the garden up. There are many mice and voles living in the garden and when Bess gets the scent there is inevitably a hole in the lawn or flowerbed. She also digs into the gravel around the house and on the drive and it is tedious shovelling it back again. She hurtles up and down the

Caught in the act, in the geraniums.

flowerbeds, stepping on young plants and sometimes snapping emerging stems. I once watched her sit down right on top of a beautiful clump of daffodils. Only half survived, but at least I could have a vase of the victims for the house. Spaniels and gardens do not mix. There is also the matter of Bess leaving her calling card around the garden. I absolutely refuse to shovel this up, so it is left to Simon. This means that when Simon is working away in Brussels, nothing is removed.

I wonder if other gardeners have foibles such as mine? Even if the mess is distasteful to me, I still cannot bear to clear it up, so I just live with it until Simon returns.

When we first came to this garden, my sister-in-law advised me not to have too many benches, as the whole place would look like a park. So for a few years I was mindful of this and had only a table and chairs on the terrace and a rickety old bench in the paddock. This was a huge mistake. I did not have the confidence then to follow my own instincts. Nowadays, of course, I feel confident enough to try out my own ideas and not worry about making mistakes, as all can be corrected later if necessary. So last year I decided to put comfort first and bought five benches to set in sunny and shady spots. This was the best thing I could have done in the garden. We see more of the beauty of the garden and its surroundings than ever. We have many more borrowed views from outside the garden and the best views within. We tried to position the benches in all the nicest places, moving them around until we were happy with them. And it is much more inspiring to sit and think in several different spots than just one or two. A new perspective can be all that is needed to solve a knotty problem.

I am very glad to have bought the benches now, as a friend of mine has just asked if we will open our garden for the National Gardens Scheme next year. Four gardens in the village will be bidding for acceptance to the scheme. We agreed at once as we thought it would be fun, an incentive to tidy the garden up and something to look forward to. One of the charities supported by the National Gardens Scheme is Crossroads, a charity that gives practical help to carers. This charity helped my father-in-law and me, when my mother-in-law was very ill. Although we are not opening the garden for particularly altruistic reasons, we would love to do something to help Crossroads.

I sowed a few seeds of annuals for the cottage garden this month – daisies, nigella and phacelia. I am aiming to have lots of self-seeders in the cottage garden to save money and work and to

Benches everywhere – left: in the cottage garden, below left: rustic style for three, below right: Tom's bench, right: by the front door and centre: a peaceful private spot in the arbour.

give a random, unstructured effect. They germinated really quickly in the utility room, which has a window and a radiator and which I use in lieu of a greenhouse. So I potted them on into 2-inch pots. When I ran out of small pots I used loo roll centres instead. As long as they are tied together in a bunch they do not fall over when I water them. Geoff Hamilton would be very proud of me.

We found a bird's nest in the bramble and holly by the conservatory. There are several small, bright, blue eggs in it, maybe a dunnock's. It is the first nest I have ever found still containing viable eggs so I am very excited about it. There is a

This abandoned nest was snapped up for £1 at the garden open day.

lot to be said for leaving a few rough patches in a garden. I hope we have not disturbed the birds too much, as I would hate it if they abandoned the nest. However, I think that my father-in-law's dog, Bess, is bound to disturb the nest, as she roots around much more these days. In fact, Bess has already disturbed a blackbird's nest in our woodshed. There were two lovely little blue eggs in the abandoned nest. But I am sure the parents will make another nest quickly enough. And for the first time ever there is a nest in the entwined rose and honeysuckle against the front wall of the house. I have been waiting for such a long time for this to happen that I am delighted. There are several other nests in the hedges around the garden, but because of the dog I fear for their safety.

I love May and get very excited about the emerging plants, the blossom, the birds' nesting and the lovely weather. The countryside around the house is so pretty at this time of year and we go for plenty of walks to see what is new. The bluebell wood near our house is an

Cow parsely in the lane.

especially favourite walk. Bess loves walks in the wood too. She spends her time burrowing into rabbit holes and ferreting

Bess is always muddy after a walk in the bluebell wood.

pheasants out of the undergrowth. And we always put the garden umbrella up in May and sit out often. All we can hear is birdsong and lambs bleating. It is idyllic.

At the beginning of May I am always gazing out of my bedroom window at the beautiful blossom around the arbour. I can see two amelanchiers, which are absolutely stunning, a pure white spirea 'Bridal Wreath', two gorgeous *Viburnum burkwoodiis*, which I pick for their scent, two pinky *Viburnum tinuses* and two frothy damson trees. By the drive the exochorda is exquisite, flowering through lavender, alchemilla and a fothergilla. I love its lax habit, though I

40

Above left:
damson blossom,
far left:
amelanchier, left:
spirea, above:
spectacular apple
blossom in the
paddock and
right: exochorda
with *Alchemilla
mollis* and
*Lamium
maculatum*
peeping through.

think it might climb if given some support.

A week or two later I look out on fabulous apple blossom. I just cannot stop taking photographs of it. The large apple tree in the paddock is spectacular and we walk down there four or five times a day to breathe in its beauty. Then come the choisyas and philadelphuses, *Viburnum plicatum mariesii* and all the elders. May is definitely the month for flowering shrubs in my garden.

This year we noticed oak apples for the first time on the oak trees in the paddock. They are very lovely but also very curious. The old walnut tree with its silvery bark is also strange and interesting in its lovely, bronze foliage and with its tiny blossom. I doubt there will be any walnuts on such an old tree, but as usual I live in hope.

Oak apple and walnut foliage on the kitchen table.

There are also plenty of flowers about and therefore insects

and butterflies. There are some painted ladies and little, white orange tips and I have already seen several, small tortoiseshells on the geraniums. The bumblebees gorge on the evergreen wallflowers and the rhododendrons are also covered with bees. Bess and I often sit watching them, eating our sandwiches and basking in the sunshine. The garden is buzzing with life and zing.

In the flowerbeds the forget-me-nots look lovely, contrasting with groups of pure red *Tulipa greigii* 'Red Riding Hood'. This is a short tulip with burgundy veined leaves, which lasts a whole month. And when it dies the flowers do not drop off, they just curl up into little red dots. The earliest geraniums *G. macrorrhizum* and *G. phaeum* are in flower now, combining with dark purple aquilegias, evergreen wallflowers in shades of pink and purple and bright purple alliums. The solomon's seal has begun flowering, providing height and stature to the borders; everything else is still fairly low at the moment. The whole look is vernal, bright and fresh.

Opposite below: splashes of colour from *Tulipa greigii and forget-me-nots*, below: spectacular colour from *Allium giganteum*, bottom right: ceanothus and centre: *Geranium phaeum* and *G. macrorrhizum.*

The cottage garden is looking lush now, too. There are yellow poppies, pink and white saxifrages, primulas, polyanthus, white iberis, violets, violas and a peach japonica flowering now.

Primulas, polyanthus, poppies, saxifrage and white iberis running riot among the higgledy-piggledy paving in the cottage garden.

At the start of the month I made a list of jobs to do in May:-

 feed everything with pelleted poultry manure and blood, fish and bone

 mulch beds with compost

 weed

 stake tall plants

 prune forsythia, lonicera, budleia (if not already pruned)

 mow lawns

 edge lawns

 paint garden benches with preservative

 cut back *Geranium phaeum* (I always leave this too long)

I am proud to say that I have done everything except painting the benches and the pruning. But there is always next month.

45

JUNE ~ *Bees*

Opposite: Early
June fills the
garden with
brilliant greens
and splashes of
colour from
geraniums and
alliums.

A FRIEND IN OUR VILLAGE has a lovely garden, which is at its best in June. So every June he has a party. It is the social event of the year for me, as I love strolling around the garden seeing what works, what I might try, what has changed over the year. Our garden does not particularly have a best season. I am aiming for year-long flowering – lots of evergreen edging plants so the beds are never bare, bulbs for each season underplanting a succession of perennials, some shrubs for structure – in all, the usual aims for a garden which is overlooked by all the windows in the house. In fact, until the yew hedge matures the whole garden can be seen at once from the bedroom windows. So though we have no best season, the garden looks fairly good all year. This means we can have lots of parties whenever we like!

Whenever we go into the garden in June the only noise we can hear is the buzzing of bees. There are thousands of them. I always associate June with bees. They completely drown out the birdsong. They especially love the ceanothus by the front door. They also love the kolkwitzia and limnanthes, but really they are

Ceanothus with
Azara microphylla,
very popular with
the bees.

spoilt for choice. There are so many flowers out in June that to list them all would be an endless task.

In the cottage garden, May flowers are giving way to white daisies and yellow aquilegias. There are still plenty limnanthes and yellow poppies and it seems to me that a yellow and white theme has developed. This is despite my intentions to have multi-colours and stuff everything in randomly. There is one pale, orange poppy that looks incredibly out of place though and will have to be moved. A friend came to visit last week and said that I really should decide on a colour scheme for that area! A polite way of saying the poppy must go. So I realise that my hotchpotch needs some order imposed on it. I will be sorry to see the poppy go though, because it is a very special one with flowers all the way up its stem and silvery, furry leaves. And as usual, I have forgotten the name.

There is some pink in here too, as when we first arrived there was an enormous pink lupin, which I disliked for its dull colour. I tried to dig it out but the roots are too deep and surrounded by immovable rocks. I think there used to be some sort of farm building there years ago. So then I poisoned it with gallons of glyphosate – twice! But still the lupin persisted. So in the end I had to accept it and I planted two pink rock roses and a *Rosa* 'Ballerina' to tone it down. Now I am glad I did, as the spots of pink look very pretty and cottagey with the yellow aquilegias and white daisies.

Aquilegias, rock roses, *Rosa* 'Ballerina' and foxgloves in the cottage garden.

We have not done much hard work in the garden this month apart from weeding the vegetable patch, which could not be put off. But we have done lots of smaller jobs. Today, I spiked the smart lawn inside the flowerbeds, to allow water to penetrate more easily (though I am sure we will not have a drought) and to aerate it a little after the storms. We are always quite careful not to walk on the grass after rain, but I still spike the lawn regularly to relieve compaction. I also sprinkled sharp sand over the lawn after spiking it, as this helps with drainage.

I have also put some lambs' litter on the flowerbeds to deter

our monster rabbits. It seems to be working so far. This was a tip from a friend who works with sheep.

I also trimmed the little yew hedge around the flowerbeds, as it has finally, after three years, started growing well. I am going to trim the sides again in September. I am so eager to have a tall, bushy hedge there that I religiously follow all the advice in my *How to Grow Hedges* book. But it does say in the book that the expected height after ten years is just 6ft, so I am prepared to wait. We usually lose two or three trees each year and do not really know why. Yew will tolerate shade and pollution and is long lived, so it is a strong plant. Of one hundred trees originally planted, I think we lost a quarter. First I thought of vine weevils, as there were one or two small, white, sluglike creatures in the roots of one of the dead trees; then I thought I had watered them too much the first year, as I read that yew hedges do not like too much water or poorly drained soil. Perhaps I did not add enough grit to the clay? But then a friend took two of the supposedly dead trees and planted them in his wood, where they revived. This is a lesson to me to give things a chance. Some things really do come back to life later on. His theory is that they were root-bound. Hmm, if so, why had some of the yews done so well? After all, they were all planted in the same way.

I finally pulled the forget-me-nots up and found thousands of weeds hiding there. We really must reduce the forget-me-nots even more for next year. But there is a silver lining: the forget-me-nots keep everything so moist that there are always a few sweet, little frogs in there as well. Once I found two copulating frogs, I actually had them in my hand with a pile of dead leaves. I dropped them pretty quickly, I must say. They did not seem to mind and carried on, oblivious, for another hour or so!

I have just staked the peonies with rusty iron supports. The supports cannot be seen, but if they ever do show because of vigorous deadheading and suchlike, I know they will look wonderful. These supports are half circles on two legs, my favourite kind. They are unnoticed when the plants are in bloom and attractive in March when the plants are cut down. But today I found some even lovelier, rusty, iron plant supports in a magazine. They are 4ft long poles with balls or *fleur de lys* on top. I ordered six immediately. A luxury I know, but I just could not resist. These will be placed in clumps of delphiniums. I always leave supports in-situ, as I love the workmanlike look of them and it saves time and storage space. Why take them out in winter

Peony 'Sarah Bernhardt', above, and a striking blue delphinium with a *fleur de lys* stake.

only to put them back in spring? Some of my supports are link stakes, which I use for taller plants such as physostegia, which can be blown down in late summer as they are quite whippy, even though they make large clumps. Because the dog jumps joyfully through the geraniums I now have to put link stakes in there to stop them being flattened. I also like the iron, circular grids on legs for bushy, floppy plants like geraniums, but as they can be quite expensive I only have one or two of these. Other gardeners advocate twiggy hazel as being unobtrusive and a perfect support. But really, I have neither the hazel nor the time to cut it and I do not suppose many people have. Even so, I am sure that if I were to use them, my twigs would be bound to snap!

A young *Crambe cordifolia* does not need staking yet.

There were some gorgeous, fat, mullein moth caterpillars on the verbascums this week, so for a few days I went on caterpillar patrol removing the little munchers. I always put them on the nettles in the lane. I hope they cannot crawl back from there.

I am also moving plants around that are not in the right place, e.g. some small campanulas behind large penstemons. One of the white campanulas did not survive this year as it was too close to and overshadowed by a lavatera.

Left: Verbascums, beloved of caterpillars.

The foxgloves are dotted about as I allowed lots of self-seeding last year, so I am transplanting them all into just three large groups. I find that in the herbaceous borders foxgloves are large enough to look as imposing as delphiniums when planted in quantity. We also have a lovely, perennial, yellow foxglove in the cottage garden. This is stunning and lasts much longer than the ordinary biennial foxgloves. I am hoping to split it next year.

Above: White foxgloves with purple salvia.

Above right: With *Rosa* 'Ballerina' peeping through, the perennial foxglove is set off by the dark leaves of the holly.

In the arbour the things we originally planted died, so I have now bought a ceanothus, two clematis, a 'Rambling Rector' rose and an akebia (an experiment as I do not know it, and yes, it is an impulse buy).

All the lupins have blackfly so I have pinched the tips out. I usually have to do this twice as there are always a few hiding in there ready to climb up when I am not looking, but as we only have seven white or pink lupins, this only takes a few minutes. I also deadheaded some of the delphiniums. A friend of mine has just given me some nepeta and a lovely, tall, pale blue geranium, which will go very well with the lupins and delphiniums, so I am very happy at the moment.

There is enormous bird activity in the garden this month. I saw a yellowhammer and had to look it up in my bird book to make sure. I think it is only the second time I have ever seen one. The cock pheasant jumps up onto the bird table in the evenings, looking very comical. Woodpeckers are frequent visitors and they have now been joined by jays. Unfortunately several birds have flown into the glass of the conservatory this month, including two woodpeckers, which both died. I threw them into the field across the lane for the foxes. I shall put some more vases against the windows and hope that helps. And I also have a decorative, glass hanging, a present from my bird-loving niece, which I will hang on the most dangerous window.

The rabbits have eaten the campanulas again, *latifolia* and *latiloba*, but this encourages the plants to grow bushier later on so I am not too angry.

In the vegetable garden the strawberries are not doing well this year and we do not know why. So I have netted them to protect them from birds, just in case. But the lettuce, onions, potatoes, gooseberries, currants, asparagus and beans are all doing very well. We watered the vegetable plot once this year. I do not

Too much lettuce, too few strawberries.

usually do this as I expect vegetables to manage on their own, but in one of the dry spells a friend advised me to water to see spectacular results. So I did water, but as the vegetables all did well last year without water, I cannot really tell if watering helped or not.

In this, the last week of June, we are eating lots of asparagus and there is still more to come; we cannot eat the lettuce quickly enough and yet we go out searching for just one strawberry at a time. 'Can't win 'em all'. We now think that the mice are eating the strawberries, as we found a couple of likely looking holes. But apart from putting poison down, I do not think there is anything we can do. So we will give our strawberries another year. If the fruit does not survive, I shall take the strawberry plants out and try something else.

At this time of the year the flowers are so pretty that I am constantly taking photos. I made this one into a card.

Another picture I made into a card – although unromantically, the *Salvia turkestanica* smells like sweaty armpits!

The aconites, penstemons, campanulas and white nepeta are still going strong. They have been beautiful for the whole month and are very easy, good value plants. I am always taking photos of the garden and as the flowers are so lovely now, I have been snapping away every day. I took about ten particularly pretty photographs, which I made into cards on my computer. Then I printed notelets, cards and writing paper with pictures on. This was purely fun for me, but then I could not resist writing to my friends to show off my work.

This month Tom and I ordered a memorial for my mother-in-law. It is a brass, armillary sphere and it will go in one of the flowerbeds and be framed by the plants. We already have a stone

Pretty enough to be made into a card, the early evening light on the meadow turns the grass and buttercups to gold in June.

plinth there and the perfect spot for a sundial. We wanted some sort of permanent memorial and I think that if we had not decided on a sundial, we would have chosen a tree with a little brass plaque. However, as it is unlikely that our house will be handed down through the family, a sundial is a more portable memorial than a tree and will eventually go to one of the grandchildren, thus remaining in the family.

In memory of Madeline
1937 ~ 2005

JULY ~ *The Glory of the Garden... and Wasps*

JULY HAS STARTED WET AND STORMY. The rain battered my beautiful peonies, so when I heard there were more storms coming I put large bin bags over the peonies to protect them. It worked! But I had to leave the bags on for four days as the weather was so bad and the peonies continued to grow and became a little leggy. I have learned from the experience and next year I will use light-permeable fleece if we have more storms. We have two 'Sarah Bernhardt', which are double, pink flowers and RHS recommended and a white, double-flowered

Thanks to the storms, an over-protected, leggy peony.

'Duchesse de Nemours', which also has an Award of Garden Merit. The young foliage is bronze and the leaves are dark, semi-glossy and make an attractive, bold clump until the first frosts.

Peonies with deep purple acconites.

The topiary holly, freshly trimmed.

Mrs Cooke from the National Gardens Scheme is coming this month to assess the four gardens in the village, which are applying for acceptance to the scheme for 2006. I should be out tidying and primping and working hard, but in truth, the rain has put me off. I know now that I am not a passionate gardener. A few years ago I would have worked in the rain, but not now, not even for the NGS.

However, in the dry spells, I have edged the lawn, trimmed the topiary holly, weeded, moved some plants to better positions to fill gaps and finally cleared away a messy woodpile. In the paddock we mowed the paths and tried to build the bonfire up, so it looks like a bonfire as opposed to a heap of rubbish and garden waste. A few old pallets

Bess in the evening light, admiring my newly edged lawn.

did the trick. I finished spreading all the homemade compost, which made both the compost bin and the flowerbeds look tidier. I also put some weed and feed on the lawn. We had a huge bag of it from my father-in-law's previous house and it had been taking up space in the garage. I am not quite sure it was a good idea to kill moss just before someone comes to inspect the garden, but it is done now, so I will just hope for the best. I also pruned the philadelphus. It should have been done a few weeks ago directly after flowering, but I am often late with pruning and there do not seem to be any ill-effects.

The roses are still out now. I have very few roses as they take up too much space and can look leggy and bare when not in flower. But they are beautiful in season, so I have three 'Rambling Rectors' on the house and arbour. These have evergreen clematis and honeysuckle growing through them, so they earn their keep as a support. When they are in flower I love their frothy, cottagey look and they never have mildew or aphids or anything else horrid. In the back garden we have two yellow roses. There is a 'Graham Thomas', which keeps on flowering as late as December, if it is deadheaded regularly. It is a pretty shade of dark yellow and much loved I think, as when we opened the garden in aid of the village hall a couple of years ago, several people asked 'Is that Graham Thomas?'

There is also another yellow rose, whose name I have forgotten, which I chose for its pale, delicate lemon colour and its resemblance to a dog rose. I love dog roses. But this rose flowers

Left: 'Rambling
Rector', above:
'Evelyn' and below:
the ever-popular
'Graham Thomas'.

prolifically for over a month and then sporadically until November and has an RHS Award of Garden Merit.

And finally there are two pink roses 'Evelyn' and 'Rosamundi' in the herbaceous beds. They are both heavily scented and I love picking them for the house. I first saw 'Evelyn' in Shakespeare's granddaughter's garden in Stratford-upon-Avon and thought I recognised it as the same fragrance as the Crabtree and Evelyn perfume I wear. I would usually pick these as soon as the buds open, but as Mrs Cooke is coming, I am restraining myself. The early lilies I planted are not early up here so are not out yet. I must try to find some very, very early ones for next year. The foxgloves and *Tellima grandiflora* should have been cut down by now, but I have left them so that Mrs Cooke can see how the garden looked in June – we are hoping to open in late June if our application is successful.

Gillenia trifoliata framing a lily, whose unopened buds still look decorative.

Good news! Mrs Cooke spent about forty minutes walking around and immediately accepted our garden. She seemed happy to have it, while we were quite surprised but very pleased.

The weedkiller did kill the moss and left unsightly, brown patches on the lawn as I suspected, but I have learnt my lesson now and will never do that again!

At this time of year the flowers are the glory of the garden. There has been a lovely succession of flowers throughout July; campanulas, lavatera, verbascums, liatris, lythrum, white veronica, lilies, sidalcea, *Salvia turkestanica*, *Lysimachia clethroides*, hebe, penstemons, *Verbena bonariensis*, budleias, baptisia and anaphalis. The peonies have been deadheaded but the foliage remains, making attractive, shiny clumps. There are lilies planted below the peonies and the peony foliage hides their leggy, wiry stems. There are clumps of geraniums everywhere, showing mostly pink

The foxgloves have gone over but the poppies and calamintha still look pretty in the cottage garden.

flowers – *G. endressii* 'Wargrave Pink', *G. oxonianum* 'Claridge Druce', *G. sylvaticum* 'Birch Lilac', *G. wallichianum* 'Buxton's Blue', *G. macrorrhizum* with its pink tinged foliage and *G.* 'Johnson's Blue'. The nepeta is still going strong. All the tall and spiky plants are getting ready for August now, the eryngium, echinops and the galtonia are almost out. And unusually the perovskia, which only came out at the end of August last year, is now pale blue. The delphiniums have great presence with their huge mauve or white heads, but even though they are all tied in, the rain still broke a few of the heavier heads off. The *Eryngium giganteum* looks very stately now, even though it is still only showing silver and the

Romantic hues of silver and blue from the eryngium.

merest hint of blue. It is such an imposing plant that I would hate to be without it. And to give definition to all these billowing flowers, the yew hedge has been trimmed twice and makes a perfect frame for the flowery landscape within.

We have had so many visitors this month that there has not

Sidalcea

Salvia superba

Flowers everywhere you look: the left bed...

and the right bed

Campanulas

66

Lilies

Left: The nepeta
tones beautifully
with the budleia.

Right: The
amazing blue of
the perovskia.

been enough time to harvest the vegetables at the optimum time – in other words, before everything becomes hard and stringy and loses sweetness – so we will have to hope for the best. The strawberries have been eaten by mice. The raspberries are not netted because there is a little blackbird who helps himself and I would not like him to become entangled in the netting. It is a race between us to see who can get to the raspberries first. The new potatoes and first earlies were the size of bakers! This is not what I wanted at all. But the names on the labels washed off in the rain and I cannot remember which varieties they are, so I do not know which ones not to order again. It would have been better to have written the names on a plan in my notebook. I will do that next year.

The broad beans are doing well. The lettuce is growing too quickly and prolifically for us to eat. We always plant too much, so I usually give it away to friends and neighbours. I can see now that we have too few onions this year. But last year we had too many. The shallots are doing very well, yielding four or five times their original weight. But they are enormously fiddly to peel, they made me cry when I chopped them and it took me forever to pickle them, so I will definitely not be growing them again. The basil is growing beautifully on the windowsill and the parsley outside, which is just as well, as we are just running out of last year's basil and parsley in the freezer. There is a glut of beetroot as usual. I do not think we will ever get the hang of, or have enough time for successional planting! Am I alone in this? Or does anyone else have more ambition than time? And finally, the apples are just getting some colour in them. There are very few damsons or apples this year. Last year we had at least 100lb of damsons and made damson wine. But we had an early frost this year, so I did not expect much fruit anyway.

I did something exciting and daring this month – I took such good photos of the vegetable plot that I sent 'before' and 'after' shots to *Gardeners' World* magazine to try to win some cash. If you have a letter and a photograph printed on the letters page, you

can win up to £100. A couple of years ago my mother came to
dig the potatoes for me, as I had hurt my back shovelling gravel
around the drive. One night we sat down with a bottle of red
wine and my mother started telling me funny stories about the
people on her allotments. We thought it would be fun to write to
the gardening magazines and tell everyone. Fortunately, we
thought better of that or we should have been sued for libel. But
the idea of writing to a magazine to win a prize had taken hold,
so we each wrote a letter to see which of us would manage to
have it published. One letter was about an article from the
magazine, which I had used to order some special plants and the
other was about allotments. It was great fun, as my mother was
trying to write her letter very neatly and kept making mistakes
with the Latin names. I think she had to write the letter out
three times in the end. However, her efforts were not in vain as
both our letters were printed and we received £20 and £25
garden centre vouchers and I was also sent a packet of trial onion

Lettuce at its
most decorative.

Not enough onions!

Prize-winning courgettes… in a photo at least.

seed. So I am hoping I will be lucky again with my vegetable plot photos.

Lambs got into the garden four times this month. Luckily they were spotted immediately and turfed out before they could gorge themselves on my flowers.

In the meadow there are hundreds of brown heath butterflies and some, whose name I do not know, with mustard spots, on the grasses. They seem completely at ease with us as we walk by. There are only grasses in the paddock as it is grazed. But next year we are going to try to have daisies and mallow in there too. The sheep never eat all the grass, so I think it is worth a try. I got the idea from Hampton Court, Hereford, which we visited a few weeks ago to look at the vegetable garden. It is very formal, in the Dutch style, I think. But on the way from the carpark to the gardens is a small area of meadow flowers. It was so pretty that I decided to try it at home. The butterflies will love it.

But the wildlife making its presence felt the most this July is wasps. We had four wasps' nests in the garden this year, which all had to be removed. We have had nests in the bird boxes for several years, but this year there were two in the ground, one in the hedge and one on the roof next to a window. I had naïvely thought that as long as you do not block a flight path or entrance to the nest, the wasps would not sting you. But one day I was digging in the flowerbed about nine feet from the entrance to one of the nests when suddenly, where there had been no wasps at all, I was surrounded by dozens of them. My first reaction was to stand perfectly still so they would not think I was attacking them and therefore would not sting me. But this marvellously optimistic plan was flawed and I was stung several times in a few seconds. I think you should only stand still with bears. At this point I ran indoors for cover and shrieked for Simon to bolt the doors behind me. The worst part was trying to get them all out of my hair, as they were merrily stinging my head and neck. Luckily I suffered no ill-effects apart from mild shock and we had all the nests removed the next day. I had hoped to save the nest in the hedge, but unfortunately could not. The pest controller told me that wasps multiply extremely rapidly and become very dangerous within about six weeks of beginning a new nest. The burrows extend several feet underground and there can be many thousands of wasps in a single nest. So now I am looking forward to August, butterfly month, as butterflies do not sting.

The golden marjoram draws the eye in the cottage garden.

AUGUST ~ *Butterflies*

THE GARDEN IS AMAZING! I have been lying in bed with a very
nasty flu bug and boredom has got the better of me, so I
ventured into the garden just now to sniff the air. I opened
the door and a crowd of butterflies flew up around me.
Then two beautiful peacock butterflies immediately
landed on my arm. What a welcome! A tip to get
butterflies to land on you is to wear a bright, fluffy,
white dressing gown when you have your morning
coffee in the garden. It never fails.

It is budleia time and for the past week the
garden has been full of butterflies. Cabbage whites
were the first to show, followed a few days later by
peacocks and then all the others seemed to arrive at once. I
found 57 peacocks on one budleia before losing count. We
have peacocks, red admirals, cabbage whites, frenchies, painted
ladies, tortoiseshells and brown heaths. I planted butterfly-
attracting plants especially for this time of year. There are various
budleias, three different sedums, *Scabiosa luccida* and various asters.
The butterflies also love *Lysimachia clethroides*, which I did not
know when I planted it.

Though I have been in bed for a few days, I get up from time
to time to look out of the window. It was rather windy yesterday

Left to right:
A red admiral,
brown heath,
painted lady and
peacock.

and I noticed lots of fluffy, white seedheads flying by like snow. When I went to the window to investigate, dozens of cabbage white butterflies were also flying around looking like snow! The effect of the seedheads and butterflies was so striking that I will not easily forget it. I love this garden!

As I lie here in bed I can hear the wind in the trees. It is a very rustly, bustly, busy sort of noise and very cheery. The garden can even cheer me up in my sickbed.

The last few weeks have seen rain just when we wanted to mow the lawns, so the grass is very long now. But next week we will have visitors from a local charity for the disabled expecting cream teas and a tour of the garden, so we will have to tidy up and mow this weekend, even if the grass is wet. I have set aside two days for this, but I know something or other will interrupt us as usual, so I will probably be weeding when I should be whisking the cream. Do other gardeners do things at the last minute, I wonder? I think garden openers must, because our weather is so changeable that we cannot always work to a schedule. And no matter how many times you weed a bed, you know there are weeds hiding in there that you will only spot on the day you open.

Before my parents-in-law came to live here, I had to think about disabled access, specifically wheelchair access. Although my

A butterfy-attracting plant, scabious is popular with many other insects.

mother-in-law would eventually have an electric wheelchair, at first she was self-propelled or pushed. So the first thing to do was to remove any steps and make ramps or slopes to allow wheelchair access to various parts of the garden. We removed two railway sleeper steps leading off the drive to the back lawn and brought in soil for a small slope. We also made a wheelchair path in the same stone as the terrace, all around my parents-in-law's side of the house, from French window at the front to French window at the back. Then my mother-in-law could get from the house to the terrace and from there to the garden. A man from the local council's Wheelchair Team visited the house to check that the path was wide enough – it was, four feet wide – and he told us to build up the level of the ground at either side of the path, so that the wheelchair would not fall over the edge. We brought in a couple of tons of scalpings and rammed them down to make a hard surface, which was then covered with gravel to match the drive. We were told that an electric wheelchair weighs about ten stone and if it overturned the consequences could be very serious, injuring or even killing someone.

The next thing was to keep the lawns closely mown to make the grass drier and the soil harder, in order to make it easier to push the wheelchair. There is nothing more frustrating than trying to push a wheelchair through wet grass and boggy ground. It is impossible unless your last name is Schwarzenegger. I began by spreading sand on boggy patches and brushing it in with a besom broom. This made an immediate difference to the drainage of the heavy clay soil. And after doing this again once or twice throughout the year, we could walk on the lawn in January without getting bogged down. At last, we could put the rowing boat back in the shed.

The lawns had only ever been mown once a fortnight and were very bumpy. I had been filling the hollows with spare soil for the past few years, but my priorities had been the flowerbeds and keeping the rest of the garden tidy. But to level the bumps and to keep the grass short all the time for the wheelchair, we now needed to mow every week, so we were very lucky to find a friend's teenage son who was willing to do this. After my mother-in-law's death we kept him on for a couple of months, as we could see the improvement and liked it. Now the lawns are much more inviting to walk on than the previous long, wet grass. And I will not mind if it all turns brown in hot weather – less mowing!

As we needed more places for my mother-in-law to sit and enjoy the views, I had also decided to make a 'wheelchair route'.

The very first fruits on our new apple tree.

This was a short row of fruit trees leading from the terrace to an arbour enclosed by circular beds, where she could sit and look at the hills 40 miles distant. We wanted half-standard or bush trees, which would not dwarf the house and would be easy to harvest – no hanging onto rickety ladders for me. And I wanted some self-fertile varieties to be absolutely sure of getting some fruit. One cannot always rely on labels. In the event, one tree did arrive unlabelled and I never found out what it is. After some deliberation we chose M26 rootstock so the trees will not grow over nine feet and I pruned them to have a four and a half foot trunk.

There are five apples, one of which is 'Red Falstaff', self-fertile, a good pollinator and a heavy cropper with beautiful blossom. Another apple I could not resist is called 'Scrumptious'. It was described as 'fragrant and honeyed, licorice and wine, truly scrumptious, soft and delicate, a bunch of cherries, crisp and sweet, ummm! and aromatic'. Who could resist? There is a damson 'Shropshire Prune', which stands opposite an existing damson and lastly a self-fertile Victoria plum. We love our fruit walk, which though young, has already produced fruit to pick at wheelchair height.

The arbour itself was made to my specification. It had to be informal as it is at the furthest point from the house and close to the rough paddock, so I chose larch poles for a rustic look. It had to be wide enough to accommodate both a bench and a wheelchair. And it needed to be high enough not to have wet honeysuckle dripping on Simon's head, as he is rather tall. I decided to have open sides so that my mother-in-law could be as close as possible to the flowering plants either side and have no obstruction if she wished to touch the plants. We made circular beds around the arbour to have an enclosed space, with a sheltered and protected feel. One day, when the shrubs have grown, I hope this will be an almost secret garden. This area was all lawn last year when we began to dig the circular beds. We did not have time to kill the grass by covering it with thick layers of newspaper, cardboard and mulch, which is what we usually do for shrub beds, so we did it the hard way – digging the turf out by hand. The shrubs were all transplanted from the site of the new garage and all survived. There is still some tweaking to do of course, but on the whole it is a success. I am looking forward to our visitors very much and I hope that the ladies will not have any problems being able to look around the garden.

I should have moved several plants to better positions by now; the delphiniums, for example, should have been cut back, watered thoroughly, moved and fed with fresh compost ready for their second flush of flowers. The deutzia and kolkwitzia should have been cut back too. I wonder if they will flower next year? But we have had visitors at the house for two weeks and I have caught this flu bug, so nothing has been done. I should qualify this, one urgent job has been done; the *Artemisia absinthium*, 'Lambrook Silver' had blackfly, but I spotted it early and pinched it off. I would like to do more before the next visitors arrive if I can. The most important things though are the lawns and edging, then everything will look good. Even though I have not done all I would have liked, the garden looks very pretty at the moment. It is full of flowers and flowers to come, lush and

Balsam grows like a weed here.

healthy. It looks like an advert for the natural look, as opposed to the perfectly manicured, rather restrained, well-groomed look. I rather like it this way and am only usually spurred into action when my father-in-law says something like 'We must do something about the lawn'. And the grass does not need to be a foot high before he says this....

He has been making a new bench for the paddock in the last week or two. We already have a bench and table that he made, in the paddock by the bonfire. The bench is a very comfortable height, with a back that supports perfectly. He is also planning to

Tom's 'bonfire' bench and table and below right: a bench made from an old railway sleeper found in the garden.

Hannah and Renata hoping these sausages won't fall off their sticks.

Below: Renata, Rebecca, Hannah and I.

make another, more formal bench for around the walnut tree. Since we put more benches down there, we use the paddock much more every day and for parties by the bonfire.

My father-in-law Tom has a wood-turning lathe in his shed and spends several hours a week on this hobby. He made me some lovely cane tops for the vegetable garden.

I have lots of cane tops in plastic, wood, terracotta and cork. They are all slightly different and some are endearingly wobbly. He made two different ones for me – some in the shape of acorns with one hole in the centre and some in a dome, finial shape with five or six holes to hold a wigwam of canes.

July and August are months when earlier hard work in the

Handy help in the kitchen and in the garden, shelling peas and picking thousands of caterpillars off the cabbages.

The owl Tom made for us was mobbed by other birds when we first put it up!

garden pays off. Apart from mowing and a little weeding and deadheading, the garden takes care of itself and looks beautiful. I find that there is such a succession of flowers that we never need to worry too much about how the garden will look when visitors arrive. And invariably everyone is entranced by the flowers, the buzzing insects, the butterflies, the birds, frogs, rabbits and even the squirrels are delightful to them (though not to me, I must say, because of the damage they do).

We have the hummingbird hawk moth on the budleias now. Children are absolutely fascinated by them. The first time I ever saw one I thought it might be a baby bird and that is exactly what the children usually say. We are very excited about the moth, as it is such a rarity.

Visitors love helping in the vegetable garden, too. The peas, broad beans, potatoes, courgettes, onions and soft fruit all need harvesting now. The children love picking and shelling peas and beans. Peas, especially, are easy to pick at child height and shelling is fun, as they are allowed to eat as many as they like. Thanks to our visiting nieces and nephew, we have managed to freeze all our beans and peas this week.

The sacrificial brassicas.

Another job for the children is picking caterpillars off the cabbages. We put the caterpillars onto some nettles in the rough grass and hope they will thrive there. I usually hose the caterpillars and eggs off the brassicas when I see the very first ones. But this year I was away and the caterpillars have stripped the leaves. And yet, after picking off what seemed like thousands of caterpillars, we have now decided to sacrifice the cabbages for the butterflies' sake!

In a few days some friends and a photographer are coming to take photos of the garden for submission to the new gardens section of the NGS *Yellow Book*. There is a small section in the book for photos of some of the new gardens each year. I had a look and there are just 16 photos this year, so we have probably not got much hope of being included in the next book. Some of the gardens are quite grand, but one of the photos is more or less one rhododendron.

It is rather difficult to guess what sorts of photos the organisers will be looking for. In any case, my garden is very weedy at the moment and it has been too wet to mow. But my friend Angela, who is organising our village gardens' entry, is hoping that one of

Spot the multitude of weeds…

our gardens will fit the bill. She says that a photo 'hides a multitude of weeds.' I am also taking this opportunity to ask her photographer to evaluate some of my own garden photos.

I take very many photos of the garden and would like to

improve my skills, but I have not got a critical enough eye when it comes to my garden. I think I need to enrol on a photography course at our local college. Who knows? I may become the next Fritz von der Schulenberg. I have already been on a course to learn how to enhance digital photos, motivated entirely by my desire to have lovely photos of the garden. I now know how to improve colour and contrast, take three photos and turn them into a panorama and how to erase power lines and septic tank hatches from pictures. But for me, the main problem with photographing

the garden is getting up at the crack of dawn to get the best light,
or patiently waiting for the perfect moment when the evening
light casts its shadows. Somehow it seems Andrew Lawton need
not worry about hanging his lenses up just yet.

10th August – The visitors from a local charity for the
disabled came today to have lunch and stroll around the garden. It
was great fun and very successful. The elderly, not very mobile
ladies enjoyed the garden very much and commented on the
lilies, which are almost all out now, the large, white, multi-

headed, Madonna lilies being the favourites. They also loved the
bright orange marigolds in the vegetable garden. These were from
a packet that came free with a gardening magazine and I quickly
pushed a couple of seeds into the ground in May. They are tall
and very bright and clear with a lovely, downy leaf – a perfect,
though wholly accidental, contrast with the red lettuce. They
should self-seed, so I must remember to look out for the
seedlings. The visitors also loved the butterflies, which are
everywhere now. One lady enthused about the globe artichoke in
the vegetable plot and the *Eryngium giganteum* in the flowerbed, as
they seem so huge. They provide stature now and also have such
long-lasting flowers that they will be a firm presence until spring.

I made small posies for everyone to take away, comprising
white budleia, *Verbena bonariensis*, lavatera, *Lysimachia clethroides*,
sidalcea, polygonum, *Sedum spureum*, *Lamium maculatum roseum*
and *Anemone japonica*. All last well in water except the *Verbena
bonariensis*, which starts to drop its tiny flowers immediately. But
even so, it has thousands of flowers to lose, so looks good for
about four days. Simon took a wonderful photo of one of the
posies, which I love so much that I have made into my

Madonna lilies
contrast nicely
with perovskia,
while the burning
colour of the
marigolds is set
off by their
brilliant green
leaves.

screensaver on the computer.

The cottage garden has lost most of its froth of white daisies now, and it is almost a relief to have it calm and peaceful again. The origanum, or golden marjoram, looks pretty, echoing the yellow-variegated jasmine on the trellis. And the yellow Welsh poppies are having their second flush of flowers. The *Sedum spureum* is just coming into flower and the self-sown orange and yellow nasturtiums are adding brightness in the evenings, when they glow in the dusk. There are crowds of caterpillars on the nasturtiums, but they do no harm other than eating the leaves and the fewer leaves there are, the more the flowers shine out. I think the birds must be having a

Nasturtiums – nibbled but still beautiful.

wonderful time feasting on them. The theme in the cottage garden now is purple and yellow. The calamintha tones with the *Nepeta faassenii* 'Six Hills Giant', which never grows too large on the stony soil in that spot. The variegated mint has gone wild, as I knew it would, and also harmonises with the nepeta. These misty purples and muted yellows are stealing centre stage from the whites.

In the paddock, Simon goes thistle-chopping whenever he can, but seeds have blown over from the neighbouring fields like snow and have landed everywhere. We shall never be rid of the thistles, but I have a sneaking suspicion that Simon likes this challenge. How strange the jobs we enjoy – Simon likes cutting thistles and docks and chopping wood, which I hate, and I love deadheading and moving plants around endlessly to get better compositions, which he hates. We both love mowing the paddock and mowing the garden lawn at odd times when we are feeling energetic. Neither of us enjoys mole trapping, so thank heavens for my friend, Frank, who has just caught a mole in the lawn.

The penstemons were very disappointing this year. They never fully recovered from the depredations of winter. We have finally lost all the 'White Bedder' and 'Stapleford Gem'. I really must take cuttings in case of winter losses and damage. This requires very little or no space in the garden, just a few pots in the porch or by the door, so I really have no excuse.

The catalogues for autumn vegetables have arrived. I am going to try autumn lettuce under glass this year and onions and potatoes as usual for Christmas. Last year the onions were ready for Christmas but the potatoes were late. It all depends on the weather.

I love trying new things in the garden. This year we tried some fabulous, sweet squash that can be made into chips. I also pickled beetroot for the first time. Last year I froze the beetroot and it did not work very well. The thawed beetroot was slightly slimy, so I had to throw it all away. But the pickled beetroot is a huge success. A friend told me how to do it. One simply boils and slices the beetroot and packs it into jars, before pouring spiced, pickling vinegar over and sealing the jars. I did make a mistake with this however, as it was not as straightforward as I had thought. The recipe says 'Boil the beetroot for $1^1/_2$ hours, cool, peel and slice.' So far, so good. Then 'Put in jars and cover completely with pickling vinegar.' This I did. But the beetroot kept popping up above the vinegar after a couple of minutes. I phoned my mother for advice, but as she had never had this problem all she could suggest was either topping the vinegar up or removing some of the beetroot. Neither of these worked. In fact removing some of the beetroot simply gave the rest more room to float to the top. The problem, I realised, was that the jars I used had too wide a neck. They are lovely, old Kilner jars I have had for years, probably more suitable for preserves. But beetroot needs a narrower neck to hold it down (onions too I should think) and this was not mentioned in my recipe. They should bring out *Foolproof Pickling for People Who Need Explicit Instructions*. So I decided to give up and hope for the best. Mould is penicillin after all.

I also discovered that beetroot is at its best for only three months. I foolishly imagined that all pickles would keep until the

Pickled beetroot doesn't last forever, so it's a mistake to make too many jars.

next Ice Age, but this is not so. There is a limit to the amount of pickled beetroot my friends and I can eat in three months, so my next project will be to find a recipe for something I grow that will keep for a year.

I have just been away for a few days and the broccoli has gone to seed and the French beans have turned yellow, as nobody picked them while I was away. But nothing else suffered and now I have leeks, onions, cauliflower, cabbage and beetroot ready to harvest. Oh yes, the grass went wild too. I have lots of mowing to do to be ready for my birthday next month.

As my birthday is in September I planned the borders to be in flower for this month. The theme is purple with spots of white and pink. We have *Verbena bonariensis, Geranium sylvaticum, G. endressii*, physostegia, lamium, lavatera, delphiniums, *Rosa* 'Eglantine', several budleias, *Anemone japonica*, perovskia, caryopteris, echinops, tall purple sage, white campanulas, scabious, galtonia, ceratostigma, polygonum, a tall, purple plant from Belgium, some lilies, asters just starting, geraniums in leaf looking fresh, lots of insects smothering the sedum and many butterflies about. It really is a very lively looking garden in September.

Elsewhere, leaves are changing colour and falling and, of course, it is misty in the early mornings. There is plenty to harvest in the kitchen garden as well, so this really is the 'season

Scabious, above, is very attractive to insects.

Opposite: Plants are starting to seed now, but there's still plenty of colour.

Lavatera and budleia intertwined.

Hints of autumn in the shrubs by the arbour.

Above: Romantic
evening light
casting its spell.

of mists and mellow fruitfulness'. I have never felt it so much, as this year as I have been working away for two weeks in the sun on the continent. It is quite a shock to come back to colder weather and mists. It is impossibly romantic, but there it is. Even I rushed out with my camera this morning to capture September on film, but the atmosphere is elusive and intangible, so the photos look bland, colourless and lifeless. Perhaps poetry is more evocative for this time of year.

Yesterday we had another perfect day, warm and sunny, bright but not too bright, perfectly still but not balmy; we could have walked but preferred to sit and breathe it all in. It was the sort of

Lysimachia going to seed with a purple physostegia still fresh in the background.

day when we did not want to go indoors at all, but sit out even in the dark, listening to the owls.

I enjoy watching flowers going to seed in September. There are drifts of flowers now, rather than defined clumps. The lavatera is so large that it has even overtaken the budleias for once. The physostegia has flopped though. I have never had to stake it before, but while I was away there was a great deal of wind for two or three days and branches were blown down. The physostegia suffered, but fortunately nothing else did. The pink physostegia has become too rampant now, after four years in the same spot, so I am replacing it with a less invasive purple one.

I have decided to break the habit of a lifetime and actually do some work in the garden this month. I usually like to sit back in September and enjoy the garden, anticipating the birds on the seedheads later on, soaking up the atmosphere, enjoying the calm, the refreshing rain, the perfect days. But as I am going away again

in October and November, I really do need to do some work
now. This, then, is my work for three months rolled into one:-

 cut down the hebe that is blocking the view

 deadhead scruffy-looking physostegia and move it to a
better position

 enlarge flowerbeds by a foot and stack turves upside down
in the paddock

 enlarge the circular shrub beds by the arbour

 weed everywhere

plant autumn potatoes Charlotte and Juliette, autumn onions, salad and basil (this is simple enough to do, as we have small beds which are easy to work, as this year's crops have just been harvested)

 move delphiniums to better positions

 edge the back lawn

 paint the garage with creosote – the garage counts as gardening for me

 tie 'Rambling Rector' roses in to the house wall

 paint the garden furniture with clear preservative – Teak Renew

 cut lamium to the ground, as I did not manage to do it earlier

 move self-seeded verbenas

 trim the yew hedge.

As for the yew hedge, some plants are too close to it now that it has finally started to grow, so I must move them. I did not want to have everything at final spacings when I first planted these beds, as the hedge was so tiny and the perennials so small that I thought the beds would look too bare and spotty for the first few years. So I did what everyone tends to do at first and I planted very closely. But now the hedge needs space and the perennials are large enough to divide and reposition. This is a job that can be done over several winter months whenever the weather is good and whenever I have the time. But I hope to finish by April. And the slower I do this, the more settled the beds look.

I used to love the newly planted, freshly dug look and would set aside a few days in which to complete the whole project. The 'blitz it' approach! But these days I prefer things to look less chaotic. Does this reflect a calmer personality? Probably. I used to be in such a hurry to do things in the garden, but now I take my time.

I am sitting in the garden watching butterflies – my new hobby – and swallows getting ready to fly south. The ceratostigma attracts red admirals and painted ladies; I must get another one. It likes dry sunny positions, which it has in my flowerbeds. *Ceratostigma plumbaginoides* goes beautifully with rue and as I have three balls of rue I want to have more of this combination. The garden is idyllic at the moment. It is full of little squeaks, rustling and twittering and yet is very peaceful and mellow.

I always think of the countryside around the garden as part of the garden. Is that strange? The countryside is connected to the garden by the borrowed views, the overhanging trees, the weather and the harvest – chestnuts, mushrooms, rosehips, blackberries,

A borrowed view.

A seedling oak finds a home in the flowerbed.

We often get seedling trees in the half-barrel by the back door, as this is where squirrels bury their nuts.

elderberries, sloes, the kindling for the house and the wood for the bonfire. We feel responsible for the countryside; we feed the birds and we plant seedling hollies and oaks where we think they might thrive.

In September especially, the countryside becomes more important to us. We start looking for mushrooms and blackberries and at the end of the month the first chestnuts are ready. In the little wood near our house are sweet chestnut trees. We pick the windfalls up from the ground and take them home. They are somehow very exciting. Free food! Nature's bounty! They ripen fully in the house and after a few days we eat them. We have them with Brussels sprouts or in a nut roast. They are not as sweet as commercial chestnuts and they are much smaller, but we love them.

We have a soft spot for chestnut trees. The very first tree we ever planted here was a horse chestnut. We planted it in the paddock where it has room to grow. And as the neighbouring farmer's young bullocks sometimes graze the field, we put a cattle fence around it to protect it. Given our love of chestnuts, when I saw a photo of a small-garden, sweet chestnut in the Marshalls' catalogue, I had to have it. It is called Regal, will begin to crop in its second year after planting and will only reach 15 feet in ten years. It has attractive, glossy foliage and the blossom is scented.

Who could resist?

I usually experiment with autumn vegetables at this time of the year. I have tried Christmas onions and potatoes. The onions I planted in September grew well but were slightly small for Christmas, so we left them in the ground until spring. The potatoes, however, were fine. This year I am trying onions again and I planted them very early this time. I also decided to try autumn cabbage, kale and winter salads. I ordered plug plants of the cabbage from Marshalls and then went away and forgot to remind my father-in-law to expect them in the post. When I

A fence protects the chestnut tree in the paddock from these fellows.

returned there was an unopened box with very slimy plants inside. I do not know whether they will survive but they have been planted in hope. The winter salads are from seed and are doing well so far. But will they survive the frosts before Christmas? We shall see.

I asked two friends and my father-in-law to help themselves to ripe vegetables while I was away, but nobody did. So all the cauliflowers have gone to seed and the cabbages are past their best. The broccoli has also gone over. I never want to go away at harvest time again.

Yesterday I was up a ladder tying roses in. Whose idea was it to have roses growing up a wall? It cannot have been mine. This is downright dangerous, even if you have someone supposedly holding the ladder steady for you. The books all advise wearing stout gloves for this job. How exactly do they expect you to tie the string wearing stout gloves? It is impossible, as they would know if they had ever tried.

We have several lengths of unnoticeable green wire attached to the wall onto which we tie all our climbers. These go no higher than the bedroom windows as we do not want climbers in the roof tiles. I am trying to tie the roses into an arching fan shape, with the tips of the roses pulled towards the ground for better flowering. However, as the support wires are all horizontal my fan shape is very elongated. But the roses still flower no matter how much I bodge the job. The only tip I have to help with tying roses in while balanced precariously on a ladder, is to cut the lengths of string in advance and make them very long. My string is very smart. I bought it in Paris and it is green and cream, twisted around like the stripes around an old-fashioned barbershop pole. Most people go to Paris for the sights, but I love visiting all the garden shops along the Seine. You can find lovely, brass plant labels and enamel markers in these very chic establishments. My friends say you can take a love of gardening too far....

Yesterday, on *Gardeners' Question Time*, garden designer Bunny Guinness said she goes out in the evenings with a bucket of boiling water and a torch and drops any slugs she finds into the bucket. Yuk! We have no problem with slugs, as I put sawdust and ashes down occasionally because slugs do not like dry ground and I also have a bird feeder nearby. Slugs do not eat my seedlings in spring because I put them out when they are fairly large plants and throw a few ashes around. If we ever have slug holes in potatoes and cabbages, we just eat the good parts. On the same day that we got hedgehog William, Monty Don on *Gardener's World* said 'This week is slug-awareness week'. How on earth does he manage to keep a straight face? I am not particularly 'aware' of slugs, but I found a book about slugs to acquaint myself with their habits and therefore become more aware. According to my book, slugs hibernate, so if you clear the garden in spring, which I do, you will kill the the slugs while they are sleeping. And as they are very good for the compost heap and moreover, cannibals, any slugs which are still alive when they arrive on the compost heap, will stay there for a while, helping me make excellent compost by eating everything in sight, including their compatriots! One point to me, slugs nil. If you also hoe your weeds, which I do, you will reveal the slugs' eggs and they can be eaten by birds. Two points to me, slugs still nil. And if you put dry material such as ashes or sawdust on your beds, slugs will stay away, as they need moisture for their slime trails. Game, set and match to me!

Wormcasts have just started appearing on the lawn. I sometimes brush them away, but not usually. I do not mind the lawn looking a little spotty at this time of year and I know that in the spring it will be clear again. Grey squirrels, on the other hand, are a huge pest and I loathe them. A squirrel snapped a branch off one of the new, little apple trees. I watched him doing it from an upstairs window and screamed at him. It made no difference. He continued pulling apples off and stepped on a branch and broke it irreparably close to the trunk.

30th September – We saw the first geese flying south today.

– The *Lavatera Barnsley* reverted to dull pink in parts so I cut those branches out.

– My brother brought me some tulip bulbs and my neighbour gave me some roots of geranium, a cornflower and a shasta daisy.

A late September bunch.

– I dug up and split some of the galtonia bulbs and replanted the bulblets.

– In flower on 30th September: roses, teucrium, blue geranium, blue asters, *Verbena bonariensis*, penstemons, perovskia, acidanthera, delphiniums, eryngiums, tall, pink, bottle bush shrub, whose name I do not know, malva, phystostegia, hypericum, *Sedum spectabile*, cowslips and lavender.

The fothergilla has turned colour now. It is glowing! The hawthorn is covered in bright, red berries and the blackberries in the hedge are ripe and ready for the October harvest.

HAVING BEEN AWAY for two weeks, I have returned to a garden filled with beautiful autumn colour. The garden was not planned with this in mind, but we have some berries and there is lots of colour from neighbouring oak, beech and sycamore trees. However, there are a few perennials and shrubs which I did plant specifically for winter foliage, such as physostegia, a beautiful, deep, golden orange and *Sedum spectabile*, whose burgundy flowers are familiar to everyone. As this is such a valuable, late-season plant I am trying to increase it in four large clumps at the corners of the flowerbeds. If you cut sedum when it is in flower, it roots very easily in water and can be kept in the house looking good for a month or more. We also have some artemisia, 'Lambrook Silver', which brightens the beds, giving frosty, silvery glints among the other plants. I am increasing this by division and putting it close to perennials which die down in autumn, so the bare space will be covered by the lax foliage of the artemisia.

Overleaf: *Cornus elegantissima.*

Sedum, cut when in flower, roots easily in water.

Autumn colour –
below left:
*Lysimachia
clethroides*;
below:
polygonum; right:
kolkwitzia and
above right:
beech.

When we moved the septic tank, we saw that the lawn looked very bare and lacked direction. So we planted six trees for autumn colour: two *Malus robusta* 'Red Sentinel', two *Cornus kousas* and two rowans. The small red apples of the malus are very striking and Christmassy at the entrance to the paddock.

A splash of colour from the small apples of *Malus robusta* brightens a dull autumn evening.

They keep their crab apples well into the winter, have masses of single, white, pink tinged blossom in late spring and they are in keeping with the two old apple trees already in the paddock. The rowans and cornuses are just beginning to change colour. Their autumn foliage is a plummy red. I think they will come into their own in November.

An unexpected bonus this year is the shining, fallen leaves of the ash on the lawn. It is as if a modern carpet designer had planned it, it is so perfect. The light green leaves of the ash make the grass look neon green. I know I shall have to rake the leaves up, but not just yet....

Now is the time to plant bulbs and this year I am going to plant some in the paddock for the first time. As we let our neighbour's sheep graze the paddock we cannot have plants or flowers in there, as sheep always eat everything you do not want them to. But the farmer usually takes the sheep out for a month or two before lambing and last year the sheep did not use the paddock until after lambing in May. And so I have decided to try some very early miniature narcissi under one of the apple trees. I would like a very gentle, understated effect.

The alliums and lilies did so well this year that I would like to increase them in the flower beds and have chosen more *Lilium candidum*, Madonna lilies, as they grow beautifully here. I adore their scent and the fact that they have several, lovely, white flowers on a single stem. The alliums which did well are the larger bulbs like *giganteum* and *christophii*, so I shall plant several more this year. The *caeruleum* and *schubertii*, which I tried for the first time this season, did not even come up. Whenever I plant bulbs or anything which needs free-draining soil, I always add a shovelful of grit or

The flower heads of *Allium giganteum* are like a spectacular fireworks display.

sand to the planting hole because of our heavy clay. As the bulbs die down in the summer, to ensure that we do not damage them when hoeing or dividing perennials I pinpoint their positions with various markers. Some of these are enamel, some are slate and others are oak. I found some lovely, French, enamel ones in the Botanique Editions catalogue a few years ago. I like this catalogue very much and now and again treat myself to something lovely like copper stakes and slate or brass labels. Mail order saves on trips to Paris, so I am not quite sure if it is a good thing or not....

The main thing about marking the position of bulbs or perennials that die down after flowering is to use very long markers. I have tried smaller ones of about six inches over the years, but they get lost eventually, as three inches of stake above the ground is very easy to miss when you are throwing compost down. Then, of course, you find yourself digging bulbs up accidentally or slicing through them with your spade. So most of my markers now are nine inches or longer.

Today I cut back the foliage of the aconites and peonies, which is black and twiggy now and I deadheaded the roses and lavender. When I cut foliage back, I also spread compost around shrubs and perennials before the cold winter weather. I do not know how much it protects the roots, but I enjoy doing it. It helps the surface drainage and stops the soil below from freezing.

The poppy heads are looking very straggly now, but I cannot cut them back yet as the pheasant eats the seeds. We watch him from the conservatory window. He came back today after a couple of months' absence and demanded food at the kitchen door. This is real 'pheasant weather' – cold, frosty, misty, sunny, bright. So we have started feeding him again by putting mixed seeds on the ground feeder. Sometimes I add raisins if I have been cooking with them, a handful for me and a handful for the pheasant.

For me, October is mushroom month. I love mushrooms and now there are mushrooms everywhere, including the half-barrels next to the kitchen door. A neighbour gave me some oyster mushrooms yesterday and I had them for breakfast today. Nothing

Two of our favourite pheasants tucking in.

Mushrooms galore – one of autumn's most versatile and free foods, a gift from Frank.

could be better. Frank brings me field mushrooms as big as side plates for about six weeks from now until mid-November. I make delicious, black mushroom soup, some of which I freeze for Christmas to have with sherry, and I make white wine, cream and mushroom sauce for pasta. And, of course, some of them I sautee for breakfast. I am so lucky to have a friend like this that I have dedicated this book to him!

Some of the many wonderful mushrooms in the garden.

We have at least fifteen different kinds of fungi in the garden, not including the strange and wonderful ones that grow on old, rotting logs – some are bright orange, some white and some jet-black and evil looking. They have wonderful, evocative names: shaggy parasol, knight-cap, bonnet-caps, wood woolly-foot, Roman Shield, shaggy ink-cap.... This year we had heaps of red Fly Agarics, which was a huge draw for the children. I think that living here, surrounded by such wonderful mushrooms, has inspired my father-in-law, too, as he has carved a beautiful, Enid Blyton-style mushroom scene, with an elf reading a book of spells. It is a Christmas present for one of his granddaughters. She is a very lucky little girl and I am quite jealous.

Not all mushrooms are edible...

As there is not much to do in the garden at this time of year, it is now that I make sloe gin and damson wine. There are sloes in the hedgerows around the house and if I do not pick them myself my neighbour Robert does it for me. Apparently, you should prick each sloe with a silver needle before bottling them. Well, that is the theory. I bash them with a potato masher in a plastic bowl. Then I put them in a large glass bottle and add 2lb of sugar. This is then topped up with gin and put in a cool, dark cupboard until Christmas. The sloe gin can then be strained into small bottles if you wish.

Last year I was taking a bottle of sloe gin to a friend when the bottle exploded in the car. I had not been careful enough sterilizing the bottles and must have cooled them too quickly. This time I think I shall just strain directly to my glass!

Sloe gin, almost ready now…

This year, as I knew I would be rather too busy to make wine, I gave all my damsons to friends of mine, John and Margaret. It was John who interested me in making wine originally, as a few years ago he gave me a delicious and enormous bottle of his own damson wine. However, this is the recipe I use, which I had from my father-in-law. Crush 6 to 8lb of dry, firm damsons with a wooden spoon and pour on 1 gallon of boiling water. Cover with a tea towel and leave for four days, stirring once or twice. Strain into demijohns. Add 3$\frac{1}{2}$lb sugar to 1 gallon of must. Add 2lb sugar to 1 gallon in each bottle immediately and add the rest of the sugar gradually over ten days or so, until fermentation has stopped. Rack the wine and leave in the garage for a year.

As one of the benefits of giving damsons to friends is that I usually get a bottle of wine in return, I am hoping that John and Margaret are reading this….

NOVEMBER IS ONE of the most beautiful times in the garden. There are still autumn leaves and flower colour, but we also have hard frosts and lovely sunrises and sunsets. This year we have had a whole week of severe frosts. The ground is rock hard and the grass crunchy underfoot. I know better than to walk on the smart lawn in frost, but we sometimes have to walk on the lawn in other parts of the garden, especially when we need to go into the paddock. For instance, we had a wonderful bonfire party a few nights ago and had to carry trays of drinks, soup and pizza bread down there. Children and dogs were running around and the frozen lawn was crushed. I can still see the footprints three days later. Still, I am sure that all will come right in the spring and I can always spike the lawn to relieve compaction if need be.

A summer fire blazes brightly against the darkening sky.

Though with all the mice runs, voles and moles we have in the garden, I do not really think it will be necessary.

We have two or three bonfires a year in the paddock, one in summer and one in November and I also love having a bonfire on New Year's Eve if there is enough wood. We collect wood from the lane, from neighbours and from branches blown down. And we collect newspapers and cardboard boxes all year round. It is very useful to have a bonfire, as I find the compost heaps are not always large enough to dispose of woody cuttings such as budleia and lavatera. And it saves buying a shredder.

Up to this year, the only other way of disposing of prunings was to drive them to the local tip. But in September the council introduced garden waste collection in all areas, including country areas. As we are only ten minutes away from Ludlow, I think that this is long overdue. We are not exactly in the middle of nowhere. We burn the fire very hot, waiting for dry weather so as not to have damp wood and we use the ashes on the flowerbeds later on. If I have time, I sometimes scatter the ash on boggy parts of the paddock to improve drainage.

I have just read that I can still apply lawn fertiliser if I did not do so in October. The problem is that the lawn is still growing so

vigorously that it would be madness to feed it. So this year the
lawn will go without.

    The leaves are falling steadily now and the views outside the
garden are revealed more and more. Those views seem the most
important to me now. The sunrises and sunsets are magnificent at
this time of the year. We are always running outside in our
dressing gowns at inconvenient moments to take photos of views
that just have to be recorded for posterity, or for my garden diary.
Clee Hill is so clear now that we can see all the little dots of
houses on its slopes from our bed. The mist hangs low in the dale
and as we are fairly high we look down on it; it is just like being
in an aeroplane above the clouds. It is always a thrill for me.

    The field of sheep to the north is bright and sparkly with
frost and sunlight, or sometimes it is golden brown and lustrous,
with fallen leaves and lengthening shadows. Whatever the time of

Spectacular sunsets are often associated with far-off, exotic places, but Shropshire enjoys many wonderful evening displays.

day, I am drawn to the window constantly. Frustratingly, I can never quite capture the atmosphere on film. But at least I can note my impressions in my garden diary.

Inside the garden, the flowerbeds still look full, as no seedheads have been cut down. There is lots of colour from sedum, verbena and physostegia, which I grow especially for their autumn and winter colour. Everywhere is fairly tidy and there is hardly anything to do. Because the frost is so hard and beautiful

Frost-covered leeks in the winter sunshine.

The humble cabbage looks wonderful in its coat of rime.

Glamorous strawberry leaves.

and lasts almost all day, we are looking at everything in close-up, especially in the vegetable plot. The plants look sculpted in rime and the structure stands out.

The brightest berries are the red ones and we have lots –

pyracantha, cotoneaster, berberis, holly, rosehips and the tiny red apples of *Malus robusta*. I really should buy another *Malus robusta* 'Red Sentinel', as the two I have are wonderful. The little apples look very cheerful at this time of year and the autumn foliage is a glowing red, orange, plummy colour, depending on the light. A couple of days ago two sheep got into the garden, when I left the

gate open by mistake and before we could throw them out, they knocked a few of these tiny red apples off the tree. There are also berries and hips on viburnums, rowan and elders. The hawthorn berries have all been eaten. They are always the first to go. There are very few holly berries around now, yet there are still plenty of rosehips. The blackbird sits in the cotoneaster all the time now, munching away and

Sparrows love the berberis, above, and chaffinches feast on the cotoneaster, right.

the sparrows are in the berberis eating my favourite jewel-red berries. We notice the birds very much these days. Flocks of small birds fly from budleia to budleia, very chirpy and bustling. Chaffinches spend a great deal of time in the cotoneasters and wrens and pied wagtails are always around, foraging for insects. A

wagtail followed me around the garden today, singing his heart out and eating insects on the lawn. He seems quite tame.

There is nothing to do in the garden now. Everything takes care of itself for a few months. But in the paddock we have to clear fallen wood and build a new bonfire for New Year's Eve. I love making the bonfire. All year round we pick up fallen twigs and branches from neighbouring fields and lanes, but in autumn and winter after windy weather there is much more wood to collect. When the bonfire was burnt last week on Bonfire Night, we scattered the ash by the gate and around the benches, to help drainage in the most used areas. Then I raked the heap and put the unburnt wood in the middle of the bonfire. And finally we spent a very enjoyable couple of hours collecting more wood and starting to build a new bonfire.

Leaf mould time begins now. Leaf mould improves the structure of the soil so I am scrupulous about making it every year. Garden guru Bob Flowerdew says that leaves can be left on the flowerbeds to be broken down naturally. Although I like the idea of doing that, I also love putting compost and leaf mould on the garden in spring and autumn. It makes me feel like a real gardener!

Picking the Christmas holly early makes sense, since it keeps well, and the birds don't have a chance to eat all the berries!

I usually cut lavateras and budleias back by a third in November, because of wind rock in November, January and February. Inevitably I learned about the damage the wind can do by forgetting to cut back one year, before I went away in January. I returned to find a couple of large budleias had been blown over and it was quite difficult to get them to look anything other than lopsided for a while.

The weather this November has been true to form, windy as usual and we had several short power cuts this month. We usually have one or two in blustery weather, as there is very little hedge maintenance done by the power companies and there are very many trees in the lines. But as we have wood burners and a gas cooker, we do not suffer. And when we built our new garage we installed a generator, so we no longer have any problems with food in the freezer thawing out or the automatic garage doors not opening!

But once, we had a power cut of nineteen hours. When I rang the electricity company to ask for my £50 compensation for a power cut of over eighteen hours, the chap told me that there was an exemption clause for an 'act of God'. As I was just drawing breath to rage about windy weather not being an 'act of God', he very quickly said that in our case, we would receive compensation. The money covered the cost of the food in the freezer, but I hoped that my compensation claim and those of our neighbours might encourage the electricity companies to improve their routine maintenance. Somehow, I think that paying out a little compensation is cheaper for them….

We found a mouse's nest in the log pile and another one in Simon's wellington boot in the garden shed. The wellington was

full of seeds and nuts that the mouse must have been collecting for weeks. And we saw a field mouse on the lawn by the back door today, reminding me to bait a trap to put by the kitchen door, so I will know straight away if mice manage to get into the house this winter.

This month I cut holly and rosehips to put in buckets of water in the garage for the Christmas decorations. If this is not done by the middle of November, the birds will have eaten all the berries. Holly can be left in a bucket of water in a cold garage for up to two months with no ill-effects, so I like to cut it early.

By the end of November I feel quite comforted by my stores – potatoes in the shed, beans, peas, mushroom soup and so on in the freezer, sloe gin and damson wine all looking good and foliage, pinecones and berries all ready and waiting, like me, for Christmas.

DECEMBER ~ *Christmas Decorations*

THIS IS THE TIME OF YEAR when I am very busy making Christmas decorations. It is great fun, if you have the time, to make striking and unique decorations using dried seedheads, berries, ivy, pinecones, evergreen boughs and suchlike. This year I have allium seedheads, globe artichoke flowers, dried thistles, eryngiums and echinops. And the decorations are not complicated at all, requiring very little skill, which is just as well, simply a couple of hours, a friend or two and a glass of sherry (optional). The dried flower decorations can be made well before Christmas.

My most successful decorations this year were the allium seedheads. The globes of *Allium giganteum* are as big as footballs and make a huge impact sprayed gold or silver. I mixed these with smaller *Allium christophii* seedheads. I bought some transparent thread and some gold and silver thread and hung

A snowy patchwork – a Christmas decoration all on its own.

Opposite: *Allium giganteum* make as much impact as Christmas decorations as they do in the garden.

128

them all in the conservatory, where they sparkle and glint at night. I am so pleased with them that I gave some of them away to friends. In fact I like them so much that I am going to leave them up all year!

Usually I also do three or four candle and fresh foliage arrangements using oasis, which should only be made a week or two before Christmas. For these I use holly and ivy and chopped-off bits from the Christmas tree (we always have to cut

some branches off, so that it fits under the staircase). I love using the cream variegated holly from the vegetable garden as it goes wonderfully well with my large, creamy church candles. And this holly is always full of berries, which is a bonus.

Continuing the theme of Christmas decorations, we have strung tiny lights through the viburnums and willow near the entrance gate and will not take them down until the afternoons are lighter. It is fun to come home at five o'clock in mid-winter, down our dark lane, to the gently twinkling fairy lights in the drive.

December began very wet; we had rain for two days and two nights. I threw some bread onto the lawn for the birds in a particularly boggy spot and surreally, it floated above the sward! This is now happening less and less though, as I regularly throw

ashes from the wood burners onto the lawn and the drainage is gradually improving.

December is usually too busy for me to do much in the garden. I have been weeding at odd moments; I protected the artichoke with a straw mulch; we trapped a mole in the strawberry bed and a friend pruned the young apple trees for me. I was also about to put grease bands on the new trees, but the trunks are so small that the job would have been incredibly fiddly, so I left it. I do not think we get codling moth here much anyway....

Several plants are still flowering - lavatera, roses and penstemons – but they seem unnatural somehow. We need more berries. I made notes to myself to plant more pyracanthas and hollies.

This year two friends from the Czech Republic are staying for Christmas and New Year and we have all been busy collecting more wood for the New Year's Eve bonfire. One of them,

Martin, last visited us in January 2000 when he helped us to clear the garden. He came for a break from the pressures of his office job and wanted to work outdoors to relax. He spent a whole day in the paddock dragging wood to our first ever bonfire. His philosophy on fires was to make a small fire, light it and then feed it constantly with more wood. Simon's philosophy was to make a big bonfire, light it and leave it alone. My philosophy, as I noted at the time, was to light the bonfire and sit by it with a glass of wine in hand! I cannot say that my philosophy has changed much over the years. This year we will be having sloe gin from last year's harvest at the bonfire. This is a bottle which managed to lose itself at the back of the pantry. We shall also bake potatoes from the garden if the weather is not too cold. Last year a bag of potatoes was dumped at the edge of the bonfire and somehow were not burned. Unbelievably, they rooted and grew edible potatoes this year.

A trip to the garden centre for an evergreen swag for the banisters has resulted in an early Christmas present for me, a soil analysis kit. So this week I analysed the soil in various parts of the garden. This is easy enough to do and the kits analyse acidity, potassium and nitrogen. The soil I chose came from the flowerbeds, the vegetable garden and the arbour. I have always added whatever organic matter I can get hold of to the soil; shop-bought compost, home-made compost, tons of sand, lambs' litter, pelleted poultry manure, ashes, sawdust from my father-in-law's lathe, leaf mould, wood chippings and horse manure. Gradually, the soil is becoming easier to work and plants grow well, but I have always wanted to know the effect of all this organic matter on the ground. Sometimes I have been warned that the builders' sand I add to break the clay up will ruin the garden, but according to the analysis our soil is absolutely neutral everywhere. So there!

On this visit to the garden centre I also wanted to buy lily bulbs, both to plant in the garden and as gifts for friends, but they were sold out. So I phoned my mother to ask for white lilies for Christmas. With luck my brothers will ask her for ideas for my present and I will be inundated with lilies on Christmas Day. I can hardly wait.

JANUARY ~ Disaster Strikes!

DANCING AROUND THE SITTING ROOM at New Year has resulted in a torn Achilles' tendon, my leg in plaster for two months, a further month or two of a boot and brace – a huge ski-boot contraption that goes all the way up to the knee – possible limping for a few months, six months of physiotherapy and a possible recurrence of a tear in the tendon if I am not very careful for at least a year. As can be imagined, I am devastated and have probably spent the first week in shock. I cannot walk, I cannot dig and I cannot even get into the garden without help. Now I must rethink all my plans for the garden for this year. I will need help and will need to simplify my ideas. I shall have to be very well organised if I am to have the garden looking good for the National Gardens Scheme open day in June.

Coincidentally, when I was in hospital having my leg put in plaster, the friend who is organising our village's entry to the National Gardens Scheme was also at the hospital. When she caught sight of my leg she exclaimed, horrified 'But what about the garden?' It is obvious where her priorities lie. However, I took that as an offer of help; I wonder if she could manage four hours a week?

So, to business. I have borrowed a wheelchair from the Red Cross so that I can sit and supervise. As I have never been shy about giving orders, I think we shall manage. I have had two offers of help already, from my husband and from my good friend, Frank. And three friends are coming to stay for a week before the June open day specifically to help in the garden. Any grandiose ideas I had will have to be shelved, but I can still hope for a pretty and tidy garden – and that will have to do.

The garden catalogues have all arrived this month. Usually I sit at the kitchen table, pen and phone in hand, and order something from each catalogue immediately. I can never resist those wonderful photos and alluring descriptions of superhero-type plants that will transform my garden in just one season. But this year I am curbing myself and for once doing what all the

Overleaf: The wonderful view of Clee Hill from our garden.

There is nothing to do now but plan the vegetable garden.

books advise: I am sitting by the fire (not 'curled up' though, as my leg in plaster is stuck straight out) and perusing the brochures slowly and carefully. I have decided that it would be better to save my money this year and buy plants in flower from the garden centre just before the garden open day! No one will ever know.

However, I can never resist lilies or vegetables and so I am ordering just one or two selections from the Marshalls' catalogue as usual and for the first time from the Jacques Amand bulb catalogue. It was difficult to decide which lilies to try this year. I am always tempted to try new varieties, though I know that some types do not do well for me – martagon, longiflorum and various species ones I have tried over the years. However, as there will be visitors to the garden this year I have decided to stick with oriental and regale lilies, as I know they will grow

137

beautifully here. Moreover, rather than taking any risks at all, this year I am restricting my choice to varieties with an Award of Garden Merit. I have decided on 'Casa Blanca' – oriental, with large, pure white flowers in August at 4ft; 'Montana' – oriental, white with a rose tinge on the reverse of the petals, also 4ft in August and white regale lilies with rose purple shading on the outside of the funnel shaped petals, 4 to 5ft in July.

It is easy to see why we need more lilies.

There are rarely inexpensive *Galtonia candicans* (summer hyacinth) bulbs in catalogues, but this year I am in luck. We have clumps of galtonia in the garden, which I increase by bulblets, but I would love to have some more. Galtonias are stately, August flowering, usually white lilies, with long, sword-like leaves. They grow to 4ft for me and make a good contrast with lower growing campanulas and geraniums. I have ordered a pack of 20 bulbs for

A sitting-down job – laminating signs for the National Gardens Scheme open day in June.

Stately galtonia, with eryngium and perovskia.

£8.50, which, I think, is wonderful value.

Every year I over or under-order vegetables, but this year I am determined to get it right. I am ordering only four varieties of potatoes, as opposed to six last year; we still have two sacks full in the garage. I am ordering 300 onion sets as I did not order enough last year; in fact we ran out of onions this week as my husband devours huge quantities of them (thins the blood, apparently) and the overwintering onions will not be ready for another couple of months. There will be more peas, as I ran out of them in the first week of January and fewer broad beans, as the freezer is still full of them. There will also be a mixed bag of brassica plug plants rather than seeds, as Marshalls are offering a good value mixed collection of 45 plants of cabbage, broccoli and cauliflower and I want to make life as easy as possible for myself.

Marshalls have also introduced a packet of 15 courgette seeds, five each of three varieties, which I would love to try. This is such a good idea. I always hate paying for three or four whole packets of seeds of different types when I only use five or six seeds from each packet. And new for me this year, seeds of butternut squash. Yesterday, I made a delicious and simple butternut soup – squash, onion, curry powder, ginger and seasoning, a friend's recipe. It is a sweet-tasting vegetable we use quite often, as we bake it or add it to vegetable casseroles, so I would love to try growing it for myself this year.

We have masses of salad and herb seeds left over from the summer. There are always too many in a packet for me, so I do not need to reorder those. If you keep seeds cool and dry they last for a year or two. Germination may be up to 50 per cent lower than with fresh seed, but not low enough to warrant buying more. I also have several packets of annuals, a gift from a friend, which we did not have time to sow last year. So the grand total for this year is £84.65, a saving of £50 on last year's orders. My husband will be delighted.

I have found my vegetable garden plan from last season and I am redoing it for this year's crop. I rotate the vegetables, as any gardener should, planting brassicas after legumes so they can use the nitrogen fixed from the air and left by the legumes. And I rotate the root crops too, so I avoid soil diseases. But I am also mindful of companion planting. Attached to my vegetable plot plan, I have a list of which plants like to be grown with which, and others which are poor companions. I consult this as I plan each year's crop rotation. Good planting groups are potatoes and beans; legumes and beets; legumes and marigolds; beets and lettuce; onions and cabbage; cabbage and French beans; potatoes, peas, marigolds and nasturtiums; parsley and tomatoes; chives and carrots and finally spinach and broad beans.

Unfriendly relationships include onions and beans; onions and peas; cauliflowers and strawberries; courgettes and potatoes; legumes and alliums; radish and brassicas; sage and cucumber and lastly lettuce and broccoli. I have picked this information up from various sources over the years and have long since forgotten the whys and wherefores of the chemicals, the folklore and the old wives' tales. Some plants are meant to deter aphids; some, such as basil, attract aphids; some plants have chemicals which combat fungal diseases and some plants are food for beneficial insects. I have no clue which plants do what, nevertheless I have the list and I always follow it.

This list is also where I put my hints and tips such as allowing weeds to grow between onions and nipping out broad bean tips to discourage aphids. If I read these at the beginning of the year there is a slim chance I might remember them!

We had snow in the first week of January for a few hours, gently, softly falling with no wind. I love walking through falling snow and though this time I was sitting by the fire, incapacitated, nonetheless I was very happy to be looking out at a picture postcard scene. Although it is so frustrating, being unable to go out, there are compensations.

The weather has become windier this week, so I would like to have the budleias cut back further to prevent wind rock. Some of the autumn foliage and seedheads have been blown down and the beds are beginning to look a little untidy. The vegetable garden is very messy, with weeds everywhere and I am desperate to go out and start clearing it. I have been seized by 'January fever', when gardeners get the urge to start work for the new gardening year. As there really is nothing I can do with my leg in plaster, I have successfully negotiated with Simon to hire a couple of workers for a day to tidy the garden for me. It is probably too early, it is probably unnecessary, it will probably not make much difference to the garden in the long run, but I

Untidy, but magical in the frost.

will feel happier to have the work started. And I will not be so worried about having so much to do in the spring when I can walk again.

I discovered early on that you should not plant on clay soil in winter. It is too wet for the roots. I suppose that this applies to transplanting too, spring being a better time. But sometimes there is too much to do in spring, so I always try to split at least a few plants in the winter. I find that if I add some grit to the planting hole, everything usually survives. So my helpers can divide a few congested perennials for me. I will enjoy their company and chatting about the garden to interested people, and after all, as I pointed out to Simon this morning during our heated negotiations, I have saved £50 on my seed order this year!

There are seven squirrels in the garden now, still stealing food we put out for the birds. The problem is that they constantly bury their food in the lawn where I do not want holes to be dug, they have a detrimental effect on bird populations and they damage trees. I looked on helplessly, and not for the first time, as a squirrel scratched and chewed the bark of a young apple tree and broke a young branch off completely (oh, for an air rifle). Bess's training to chase them away is ongoing. When they come up to the French windows and flaunt themselves at her, she twitches and bristles. But no sooner does she chase them away

Tall, single snowdrops are wonderful for picking, but do not increase as rapidly as the common ones.

than they quickly return to taunt her. I have just discovered that the government is planning a large cull of grey squirrels this year. The Forestry Commission does this periodically I think, to stop damage to trees. I hope they come as far as my garden.

There are some snowdrops out now in the garden, or so I have been told. I can neither see nor get to them. But Simon will pick me a bunch or two. We have two types, giant ones and the common ones you see everywhere in hedgerows. The giant ones, which are always out first, are not as prolific as the smaller ones and look out of scale, but are wonderful in vases. We bought them by mistake as bulbs and they have never done well, being quite slow to naturalise. I usually divide the others after flowering and it seems as if they are increasing by a quarter each year.

There are also primroses and polyanthuses out now, *Viburnum tinus* and winter jasmine. The autumn-flowering cherry is in blossom and the heavily scented winter-flowering honeysuckle, *Lonicera purposii*, has been in flower for about a month already.

Primroses too, make a glorious indoor display.

Viburnum plicatum and friend.

Of all the winter flowerers, my favourite is the evergreen
Viburnum tinus. Its flowers are very subtle but there are very many
of them. They are good for cutting and last well indoors. They are
wind resistant, will grow almost anywhere and make a substantial
loose screen in four years. I like the loose, cottagey habit and
shiny leaves; so many evergreens are solid and stiff and do not
sway in the breeze or reflect the light. The flowers from
November to March are a bonus. We have several different
viburnums here; *V. tinus*, 'Gwenllian' for its pink flowers; *V. tinus*

144

'Purpureum' for its red stems and reddish purple, young foliage to tone with a *Sambuccus nigra* 'Black Beauty' and a red cotoneaster on the drive; *V. tinus variegatum* for its cream variegated foliage; *V. farreri* for its white, flushed pink winter flowers and scent; *V. bodnantense* 'Dawn' and *V. burkwoodii* 'Anne Russell' for the same reason; *V. opulus* 'Sterile', the snowball bush for obvious reasons and also for its colourful autumn foliage; *V. plicatum mariesii* for its gorgeous, horizontal tiers of flat, lace-cap, white flowers and wonderful wine-red autumn foliage, and lastly a couple of the common *V. tinus* too. I did try *V. carlcephalum* and *V. carlesii* but both died. Ah, well….

We can finally see the bare bones of the garden. There has been too much leaf till now. Thank goodness we have lots of evergreen in the garden for structure and texture. The rue balls

Evergreen cotoneaster; its berries won't last long now.

are especially good at this time of year, harmonising with the sedum leaves and silver leaf budleias. So now is the ideal time to decide what to improve in the garden for next winter. I have been to the garden centre, in my borrowed wheelchair, to see what looks good now. I love the displays of plants with berries next to plants with bright, shiny leaves. I have bought a winter jasmine for the arbour and a yellow choisya to brighten up a half-barrel.

The bird table is the centre of most activity now. We feed the birds peanuts and mixed seed. I make bird cake with solid Trex, porridge oats, raisins, bread and cheese. I am sure it is a *Blue Peter* recipe. And if I have it, I add pastry for the insect-eaters as they like the fat.

As is usual for January, the weather is very cold and icy with rain and wind, and the ground is very wet. Although I do not like walking on the lawn in wet weather, this is a good time to find waterlogged areas, where sand and ashes should be thrown later to improve drainage. Of course, I cannot do it this year myself, but I can ask Simon to do it if he has time.

Today, the last day of January, Frank came to help me tidy the vegetable garden for a couple of hours. It was a beautiful day with bright sunshine and it was quite warm after an early frost. I went out to help him but could not do much, needing a chair to sit in and a stool to prop my leg on. However, it was wonderful to sit in the sun and see the work begun. Simon and Tom were helping too. Brussels sprouts and leeks were picked, several beds were weeded and dug and I tidied a large pile of canes. We all agreed that Christmas and January had been very mild this year and are hoping that February will be the same.

Above: The ceanothus by the front door, still frost-laden, and right: an unrecognisable *Cornus controversa*.

FEBRUARY ~ Moles and More Snow!

THIS MONTH ACTIVITIES DEPEND ON THE WEATHER. Hard frosts are usual and some snow, so we try not to walk on the lawns and compact them more than necessary. As I cannot hop very far at the moment, the lawns are fairly safe. But one job we always do in February is mole catching. The moles come into the garden from the surrounding fields for a month or two. We put traps down and this always works. We catch two or three moles a week with our metal, spring loaded, double-sided traps.

We used to use sonic mole scarers. These are long, metal tubes that vibrate in the soil and scare the moles away. They have a 60ft range and you must position them so there is no gap in the perimeter. You must have heavy, clay soil for these to work as the vibrations do not carry through light soil. They work perfectly in our garden, but you have to use four large batteries in each one, which is very expensive and when the batteries ran out I would always forget to change them until a new mole came through the gap and a telltale hillock appeared.

Using traps is much easier, as Frank does it for me! He is brilliant at finding the runs by poking a long cane into the ground. Once though, he decided to catch the mole the old-fashioned way and sat down at the molehill at 12 o'clock. Moles dig regularly at certain times of the day, which is good for mole catchers but not so good for moles. Sure enough, the mole arrived on time and the molehill started trembling. Frank quickly pushed a spade into the molehill to flick the mole out. Fortunately for the mole he missed, because once the mole is out you must bash it on the head with the spade. Poor mole. And talking of pests, the squirrels are digging holes for peanuts all over the garden. This drives me mad and I really have to make an effort to be more relaxed about it.

This year I have decided to try to root acanthus. We have a huge one in the flower bed, but it looks too solitary. I would like to have two more and thought it would be fun to try cuttings. It seems quite straightforward. You must lift the whole plant and

wash off all the soil from the roots. Choose young, healthy shoots approximately ¼ inch in diameter and cut them off close to the crown. Remove any fibrous roots and cut them into 3 to 4 inch lengths. Make a diagonal cut at the bottom and a straight cut at the top. Put them into pots filled with gritty, damp compost with the top of the cutting level with the surface of the soil. Cover the pots with grit or sand and place in a coldframe or frost-free spot. They can be replanted when the shoots appear in spring. You can also do this for aconites. As I cannot do this myself, I am hoping Simon would like to try it….

The potatoes for my kitchen garden arrived this week, so I put them in the shed to chit. Last year I ordered the vegetables a little later so we only started chitting in March. It will be interesting to see if there is any difference in cropping times. I decided to cover the strawberries with glass tents to see if it will bring them on earlier. I should really use cloches, but I have not bought any, as I preferred to see if home-made tents made from recycled double-glazing would work. We shall see. I am nothing if not experimental.

Striking acanthus seeds look good all winter.

On visiting the hospital this week I was told I could have a boot and brace for the next six weeks and say goodbye to my plaster cast. This initially gave me a new lease of life. It is invigorating to be able to walk around the house on the terrace and stay in the garden for a little longer each day – accompanied by the dog of course. However, the boot is heavier and more tiring during the day, resulting in general irritability and longer rest periods. Fortunately the weather this month has been so cold and changeable that the enforced seclusion has not been unbearable.

The mists, freezing temperatures, fog, sleet, hail, snow flurries, rain and wind of February have been interspersed with a few clear, bright, calm days in which to inspect the garden. I have

The countryside looks beautiful in the pale wintry light, while indoors, bunches of *Crocus*

tomasinianus, right, viburnum, above right, and polyanthus brighten the scene.

been able to see for myself what is in flower now. I asked Simon to pick primroses, snowdrops, polyanthus, viburnum, croci and catkins for me. There are one or two violas out now, but not yet enough for a bunch. The *Crocus tomasinianus,* which I planted beneath the silver birches, are spreading at a rate of knots and look wonderful there, interwoven with snowdrops and with daffodils peeping through. This crocus is a wonderful naturaliser and even lasts for a few days in water, opening and closing at dawn and dusk. I made a posy of viburnum for the kitchen table and everyone who visited me picked it up to investigate its delicious scent. A friend of mine gathered some ivy from the garden and some tiny ferns to add to a bunch of silky-soft silver buds of willow twigs and some unknown furry brown buds. And I added some winter flowering honeysuckle for its subtle, pretty, scented flowers.

The sarcococca (Christmas Box) has been in flower for at least a month. It is completely frost hardy. I have two, underplanting a climbing rose against the front wall of the house. I grow them for their foliage to tone down a startlingly bright *Choisya ternata* 'Sundance', which I planted in the wrong place. I decided to subdue it a little rather than remove it, as I usually fight shy of very bright foliage and that might be rather dull. One of the sarcococcas has a light, yellow splashed leaf. It has pink flowers and I think it is 'Hookeriana'. The other has a pale green, yellow splashed leaf and white flowers and is possibly 'Humilis'. The flowers are pretty but insignificant, yet like many winter flowers are highly scented. But the interesting thing for me is that the shiny, black berries appear at the same time as the flowers.

They are quite hidden by the leaves yet they draw the eye because they sparkle from the depths.

The snow this month was lovely. It made a rather straggly

The topiary holly, shot from the bedroom window.

Opposite: With its pink flowers, this is probably *Sarcococca 'Hookeriana'*. Below it, the black berries contrast with the white flowers of *S. 'Humilis'*.

garden quite magical for a couple of days. I could only take photos from the bedroom window, as I was laid up at the time, but I managed one pretty shot of the gate.

I went into the garden on a very windy day this week and found a spot at the corner of the conservatory which makes a wind funnel onto the terrace. We had a windbreak there a couple of years ago, but removed it to allow easier wheelchair access to the garden and conservatory. I have now decided to plant a new windbreak. There will be an evergreen *Viburnum tinus*, as these are highly wind-resistant and this will shelter an *Arbutus unedo* which, though fully frost-hardy, must be protected from cold winds when young. I have always wanted to try one of these as they have strawberry-like fruit and white, urn-shaped flowers at the same time and seem a real oddity to me. The leaves are dark and glossy and the bark is rough and brown. They grow to 30ft, but I will keep it at about 6ft by pruning. I will put a couple of silver leaf budleias close to the terrace for the butterflies and to tone with the existing ones. These will grow quickly so we can have something to give stature while the other shrubs are establishing. There will be some ground cover too, perhaps another sarcococca and a caryopteris. I would like to continue the silver theme with a hebe or rue. If I can find a silver or grey leaf cistus I would love to have a couple of those. There are

The log store alongside the garage – indispensable at this time of year.

several which are hardy and wind resistant and the papery, poppy-like flowers are beautiful.

Christopher Lloyd's obituaries have been appearing in the press for a couple of weeks now. This wonderful gardener and author died recently and will be missed very much. He was highly thought of in the gardening community and his books have been reprinted many times, inspiring thousands of gardeners. I have several of his books and my favourite is *The Well-Tempered Garden*, which I bought not least because I liked the title. I read *Foliage Plants* and *In My Garden* when I want a relaxing book, as I like the style, simple and direct and full of humour. We also have two or three plants from his garden at Great Dixter. How strange it is to read about the death of a stranger and yet feel that person's influence in one's own life.

Although I do not enjoy Christopher Lloyd's later writing as much, I think I will try to find a book about his meadow garden in his memory. I once attended a talk by Great Dixter's head gardener, Fergus Garrett, and the part I most enjoyed was about the meadow. There have been so many articles on this lovely

planting of wild flowers and rare orchids that it must have inspired hundreds of people to try it for themselves on a smaller scale in a spare corner. The trustees have launched an appeal to maintain the garden at Great Dixter and they are hoping to raise £3 million. I am certain that they will manage to find the money.

The only work in the garden this month, which was absolutely necessary, was pruning the spring flowering clematis to the ground. We only have four such clematis, so pruning and clearing the stems only takes an hour. Hobbling round the garden on crutches takes rather longer though…. We also pruned the winter jasmine before it starts into bud. Two new bird boxes were put up in the paddock and the birds have already started investigating them. Simon brought lots of wood in for fires for me. Much of the wood that blows down in the lanes around here is used in our wood burners. I have been getting used to the different burning qualities of the wood. Young hawthorn burns well, but breaks up much faster than older logs. Older logs keep their decorative outer shell much

The earliest daffodil Tête à Tête and early croci, overplanting narcissi, tulips and alliums.

longer, giving a glow much higher in the fire. Oak and ash burn long and slow and give a dying glow for a long time. Apple and pine spit and beech burns slowly. And lastly, Frank did a little weeding for me and put some compost down to dress and mulch the newly tidied bed. Clearing and cutting back proper will begin next month, if I can find someone to do it, or in April if not.

MARCH ~ *Daffodils and Mud*

SIMON WAS LISTENING TO *Gardeners' Question Time* on the car radio in late March last year and the guests were bemoaning their gardens looking bare, messy and dull at this time of the year. He came home and told me how smug he felt, as our garden still looked good. Needless to say, I felt very big-headed at this indirect compliment. The garden does not look bare at all in fact, as I enjoy seedheads in winter and I never cut the perennials back until March. Even when the perennials are cut down, I have many evergreen edging plants which I just trim, ensuring there is still something covering the soil. There is *Lamium maculatum*

Lamium maculatum is one of the best plants for ground cover all through the year.

'White Nancy' and also the common red-flowered one, which covers a large area with its silver variegated leaves; geraniums such as *G. macrorrhizzum*, which keep their pink-tinged leaves all year long; we also have a couple of *Ajugas*, 'Catlins Giant' and

Tellima grandiflora makes wonderful ground cover for the front of a bed.

'Braunherz', which keep their purple bronze foliage throughout the winter and hummocks of *Tellima grandiflora* with maple-like leaves and later on in spring tall stems with greenish, white-fringed flowers (this is my favourite for ground cover). All these except the ajuga are cut to the ground later on after flowering. The *Sedum spectabile* will already have formed new rosettes by the time I cut the seedheads back and will have made quite respectable clumps. And there are one or two plants such as rue, which need no cutting back at all. We also have miniature narcissi and tulips dotted about to give some colour. And when the yew hedge matures, it will give stucture, texture and colour, so that the garden will look good all year round.

When cutting back last year I tried an experiment with *Nepeta* 'Six Hills Giant'. I cut one of them down in the second week of February and the others three weeks later. I wanted to see what effect this would have on new growth. By the end of April all the nepetas were the same size. The one cut early grew very slowly in the cold weather – we had wind, snow, sleet and hail – and was not damaged by frost. The other grew quickly and caught up. So I am quite happy now to cut back at any time which suits me, rather than feeling I must have it all done by the end of March. From my gardening diary I notice that last year I cut all the herbaceous plants down on 21st March. The beds look

Nothing looks untidy when covered in snow.

a little untidy the longer I leave it, but the plants do not suffer at all. One year, because I was abroad in February and March, I cut everything back at the end of April. There was no difference in the flowering times at all. How do professional growers manage Chelsea I wonder, when the plants themselves have built-in timers for flowering?

Lonicera pileata looking snug in its snowy blanket.

This month we have had hard frosts and freezing weather, lots of wind and snow flurries. In fact, we have had masses of snow this year and everywhere looked wonderful, sometimes just like Narnia. It has been deep in places and has lasted for two weeks on the hills. There were many animal tracks in the snow, most of which I do not recognise, but always examine closely. I love to see

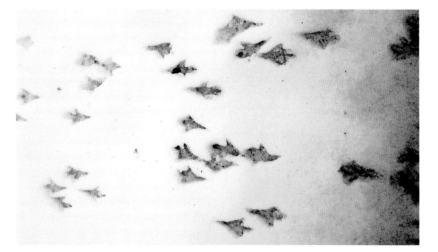

Telltale tracks in the snow.

how many creatures have been scurrying around during the night.

But when the snow melts, the garden always seems greyer, dirtier and dingier and I feel I must get some work done, but how? No-one has been willing to come and help except Frank.

He works quickly and accomplishes great things. What would I have done without him? He came to help me again today. He tidied the cottage garden and cleared the paths. There was lots of self seeding in the paths; pansies and violas, nigella, limnanthes and poppies. But with me out of action, we have not got the manpower to transplant everything this year. Most of the seedlings went into the compost, but Frank did manage to save a few pansies and violas. He also split the chives and replanted them. They pulled apart very easily by hand and he did not have to use a knife. We would like to mow the lawns sometime soon, so Frank made a start and scarified the smart lawn. The ground is too wet to mow at the moment though.

He has also prepared a new bed in the drive for planting with shrubs. I would like something to anchor the new part of the house to the garden. We had to keep the ground near this part of the house very flat, level and clear for wheelchair access. Now we can put some shrubs there and some annuals to flower this year, as the bed will look a little bare until the plants mature. I would like to plant shrubs with light leaves if possible, as most of the bushes around the drive are dark. There will probably be an eleagnus and a variegated elder with serrated leaves would be lovely too. Simon and Tom think I should go for all evergreens. But I just love elder, even though it is deciduous and I have asked the local garden centre if they would find a fairly large one for me.

My fruit book says I should apply sulphate of potash around the fruit trees now, so I have asked Simon to do it for me. We have only twelve small fruit trees so it is not a big job. I try to keep a 4ft circle of earth grass and weed free around each tree, which makes feeding easier and there is less competition for the trees' roots.

I did one or two small jobs too, but mostly directed operations. I found that even a little work was too tiring for my Achilles' tendon and I did not want to risk further injury, so I settled myself on a bench and enjoyed the sunshine. According to my gardening diary, last March I pulled a muscle doing too much unaccustomed work after the winter break. Gardening injuries are a constant theme in my diaries. There are obviously dangerous jobs such as pruning on ladders in trees; using a chainsaw to cut wood; using petrol-driven or electric machines for trimming

The valley, constantly changing from season to season and always beautiful.

hedges; using implements with sharp blades and so on. These jobs have a variety of safety accessories such as gloves and visors and in fact, I have never hurt myself doing this sort of work. But there is also repetitive work such as digging, shovelling, hoeing, spreading compost, raking, weeding and planting. This is the most dangerous for me. I may not do any weeding for a month and then have to do it all in a rush for several hours at a time. The aches and pains are endless. Gardening is a very dangerous occupation indeed, judging by my previous injuries:-

 January 2000 – hurt tendon in my left arm planting shrubs
April 2000 – tendon again, splitting snowdrops
 January 2001 – painful leg muscles, strain from digging
March 2001 – pulled a muscle in my lower back collecting
    chippings
December 2002 – pins and needles in hands and arms,
    shoulders hurting from carrying wood.
April 2002 – hurt back, pins and needles in arms for
    three days
 June 2002 – bad pain in shoulder, could hardly move head,
    shovelling scalpings

and so on until

July 2003 – slipped disc shovelling 23 tons of gravel
    around drive!

This was a serious injury. I was in pain for two months before I even had a diagnosis and sciatica had begun. Fortunately, my doctor ordered me to learn to swim the crawl to stretch my back and this cured it completely. Since then I have been much more careful. I make sure I change jobs regularly; I ask for help when lifting heavy objects; I do not dig holes for trees or remove turf any more and though I will load a wheelbarrow with something heavy, I will ask someone else to wheel it for me. I try to be more relaxed about my limitations (not particularly easy for an impatient person). I mulch much more now, to cut down on hand-weeding and I weed with a long-handled hoe whenever possible.

In my case, I often used to work away from home and so had to fit everything into a few short weeks whenever I returned. I went at the gardening with more enthusiasm than sense. Even when my muscles were telling me to stop, my head told me that all I needed was a short rest and then I could continue. Will I ever learn? Gardeners should always warm up before gardening. A brisk walk or some gentle stretching will help. Alternating tasks so that you are not simply digging for two hours also prevents strains and pain. Wearing the right clothes, lots of layers, strong gloves and goggles seems obvious, but how many times have we been cut or badly scratched because we were in a hurry, or it would 'just take a moment'? How many of us are too lazy to walk to the shed to fetch the appropriate protection? I once almost sliced my finger off when cutting some nepeta back.

Drumhead primulas are one of our earliest flowers.

But since then I have always worn stout gloves when using blades of any sort. I think I should attach a reminder about the dangers of gardening to my vegetable garden plan. Then I might heed my own advice in spring when I am always raring to go.

We have vases full of garden flowers in the house now. Flowering currants and forsythia in bud can be picked now to bloom indoors. Amazingly, *Lonicera purposii* is still in bloom. This winter flowering honeysuckle is quite a large and dull plant for most of the year. But it is evergreen and so is very useful as a windbreak on the drive. I do not find it too dull though, as its leaves are not very dark and in the summer I hardly notice it at all as I have it next to a very striking *Sambuccus nigra*. We always

Catkins and eleagnus by the gate.

have catkins indoors and also snowdrops, which are still going strong, primulas, croci, polyanthus, grape hyacinths and the evergreen wallflower 'Bowles Mauve' at the end of the month. When we have a surplus of flowers in the summer, I am not so concerned about filling the vases indoors, but in winter and early spring it is a different story. These flowers are much more desirable to me.

I usually prune the cornuses, budleias and salixes at the end of

March when the weather is good, so there is always plenty of woody material to add to the vases indoors – bright stems, sticky buds and silver leaves. I cut them down to ten or twelve inches above the ground. The budleias and forsythias flower on new wood so must be cut back and I prune the cornuses and willows to stop them from growing too large and to ensure winter stems and catkins. Sometimes I only prune half the stems and prune the rest the following year. This is what municipal gardeners on the continent do; I should think this is to avoid very stark, bare beds in public gardens.

The NGS sent me a copy of their *Yellow Book* this week. It was quite exciting to turn to the Shropshire section and find our gardens in it. But in the New Gardens section there was a photo of my neighbour's garden pond with the name of my house under it! Oh well, even if I do not have the thrill of my garden being featured, at least I get all the fame and glory…. I then turned to the website to see if my garden photo had been entered there yet, but

unfortunately not. However, as a reward for opening our garden we were sent two free entry tickets to other NGS gardens and National Trust properties. This came as a very pleasant surprise indeed and we will certainly make use of them.

The daffodils growing in the new apple walk are still coming up, even though I mowed the leaves down last year in an attempt to get rid of them without having to dig them up. This year I shall pick the flowers and then immediately chop the leaves off. Daffodils are very tough, aren't they?

27th March – Today we picked the first bunch of daffodils for

Mud everywhere; washing the main offender.

the house; it is always a thrill.

The weather this last week of March has been so windy and rainy that next year I think I will cut everything back in November and go away for the winter! There is absolutely no hope of mowing the lawns, which really need cutting, as the ground is sodden. Mud, mud and more mud is everywhere. It is hard enough walking as far as the compost heap, but we even have to wear welly boots to pick a bunch of flowers. Still, there is much more light now, which is always a relief and so energising. Simon was up at the crack of dawn today picking Brussels sprouts and salad leaves! It was a miracle! And there are more daffodils, primulas, polyanthus and miniature irises out every day. Buds are swelling everywhere and there is a real feeling of expectation and excitement in the garden. Lambing began in January, but it is only now that the farmers are bringing the lambs out to the fields. So with all the sheep bleating, argumentative pheasants squawking at each other and all the twittering that is going on, it is becoming very lively around here. I think winter may be over and spring has finally arrived.

Spring has sprung…

APRIL ~ *Spring has Sprung!*

APRIL HAS BEGUN WITH an hilarious episode of *Gardeners' World* on the television. First, Sarah Raven wanted to divide a rudbeckia, but she did not want to put it down on the flowerbed as there were young shoots coming through, which might have been damaged. So she very sensibly put it on a plastic sheet on the path. However, she then proceeded to walk all over the bed in her enormous wellies! Not once but several times! We were in stitches. Simon said, 'Bring back Anne Swithinbank', then felt guilty and said, 'No, I didn't really mean it, I think she's sweet.'

Then it was Monty Don's turn to make us smile when he said he had not got a plan for the garden – yes, he really said that. Simon said this meant he had not got a clue, but then thought better of it as Monty Don is my hero. But really Monty, saying most gardens evolve does not mean you do not have to have a plan. Don't be so disingenuous!

Early spring in the cottage garden.

Next came Carol Klein, who said 'The spring garden is at its very best now and it's going to get even better!' We were rolling about over this one. But we would forgive Carol Klein anything because she is so enthusiastic about everything. This woman could make a dark, dull, boring shrub sound like the 'must-have', absolutely perfect foil for exotic flowers.

Lastly, Joe Swift said, with not quite a straight face, that he wanted to reinvent the hanging basket! What exactly are you going to do with it Joe? We decided it must have been the April Fools' programme.

But there were several interesting snippets particularly relevant to our garden. For example, their three-year-old yew hedge was growing at different rates, as only part of it was protected by a windbreak. The protected part was five feet high and the rest was only half that height. Our hedge is a good example of the unprotected hedge, growing very variably and I am seriously considering putting up some sort of protective netting or wicker hurdle next winter.

They had also done a small trial with potatoes, to see if chitted potatoes produced a larger crop than unchitted potatoes. Surprisingly, the unchitted ones yielded a heavier crop. As the trial was so small there will be another larger trial this year with 'Charlotte', 'Sante' and 'Red Duke of York', all of which I grow regularly. If the results show that unchitted potatoes really do produce more, I will certainly not bother to chit in future.

Then an aster grower said, rather dogmatically, that you should use a systemic fungicide to make sure your asters do not get mildew. What rot! We have never sprayed our asters and they have never had mildew. Maybe if one grows a million of them in a small field one might have problems, but not many people do.

Monty Don made us smile again when he put a plastic shower cap, the sort you get in hotel bathrooms, over a tray of chilli seedlings to keep moisture in. A great idea, but what a sign of the times! Another sign of the times is the many interactive trials viewers can take part in – chilli trials, when does your tulip

flower?, pumpkin and sweet pea competitions and so on. And finally, an exhortation not to stop feeding wild birds because of fears of a bird-flu pandemic. In some countries wild birds are even being shot because of this fear, but if the virus does mutate, shooting wild birds will certainly not make much difference. What will I think when I look back on my gardening diaries twenty years from now? Will everyone have a 'jungle garden' and be growing mediterranean plants because of water shortages? We are living in very challenging gardening times indeed.

The weather has begun to be bright and sunny now. We also

The entrance to the little wood on 1st April. Brighter days encourage us to get out more now.

had a little snow, lots of hail to bash the daffodils and last night a very hard frost, all fairly typical of April. As the weather is improving, I am eager to plant seeds in the vegetable patch, but I hold myself in check until May because of the hard frosts we are bound to have and the variable weather. Onions can go in now, but when I asked Frank to plant the potatoes for me, he refused, saying potatoes need to go into warm ground.

Discovering I can hoe weeds has given me a boost and I can walk a little further every day. I noticed that one or two more support wires were needed on the front wall of the house, so I drilled the holes and managed to put them up myself. I think I can also paint the wooden garden furniture with teak oil without too much strain on my tendon. It is getting better every day.

The herbaceous borders before Frank's ministrations…

Frank cut all the herbaceous seedheads down for me this week. Budleias and lavatera were cut to 12 inches. He also did some weeding and the lawn had its first cut. I cut some

penstemons back and Frank planted the onions and broad beans.
Everywhere looks very neat after the winter now and I begin to
think that we shall manage the garden open day as long as
nothing happens to Frank....

… and after.

I am doing a little more work in the garden now, some
pruning, pulling dead leaves off primulas and suchlike. I can now
manage to take a wheelbarrow of weeds down to the bonfire.
But I also do a fair amount of sitting in the sun resting my leg.
What a glorious day today (10th), blue skies, fluffy, white clouds
and bright, bright sunshine. Even the dog seems chirpier, if you
can say that about a dog whose tail never stops wagging.

This last week has been too rainy to mow, but there are
compensations. Every night there are blackbirds and pied wagtails
on the lawn digging for worms and when it rains the garden
always looks cleaner, fresher and more vibrant. As it has been so
wet, I took the opportunity to have the lawnmower serviced.
This year I am very late having this done because I have not
been able to drive the mower to the shop. But no matter, the
shop was able to service it very quickly for me. When the mower
was brought back to me, the chap delivering it took a lovely
lawnmower off the lorry and I was very pleased we had such a

good machine. Unfortunately, that particular lawnmower belonged to someone else. Then he took ours off the lorry and it looked so small in comparison that I had to ask whether the shop did part-exchange! Luckily they did and I was able to upgrade my mower for a model with a larger blade. The new mower cuts well, is just as easy to use and does not bounce around so much on bumpy ground. I am very happy now!

April is daffodil month; they are everywhere and look so pretty. The dandelions and a few celandines are coming out too. The spring theme here is bright, sunshine yellow.

On *Gardeners' World* last night Monty Don showed us how to make our own rusty-iron, plant supports by bending steel rods to shape. It is simple and very cheap and I wish I had known about it a couple of years ago. If I can find a supplier of steel rods I would like to try this myself.

There is a pheasant with a limp in the garden now. My father-in-law is feeding him. I do not know how long he will survive with a bad leg, but the threat of bird-flu has not stopped Tom feeding the birds, squirrels and mice around here, so our little garden zoo is safe for now.

Gardening usually starts in earnest this month. One of the first jobs to do in April is weeding. Our clay soil grows many weeds, notably dock, buttercups, dandelions, clover and herb robert. The weeds that have insinuated themselves into a prized plant I usually kill with bio glyphosate, rather than digging into the plant. I use a tip I read in a gardening magazine – put a tin can, from which the ends have been removed, over the weed and spray directly into the can. This stops the weedkiller going onto the leaves of the precious plant. All other weeds are hoed, in the case of annuals, or forked out in the case of deep-rooted

It all looks tidy, but beware of weeds in April.

perennials such as docks. Gradually we are getting fewer and fewer weeds, but we have to weed strenuously in April and May or we lose the battle for the summer.

In the paddock this year there are hundreds of celandines. We have never seen them there before, probably because the grass was too long. There is also a tiny, little white flower I do not recognise and a small blue one has just begun to flower. I love wild flowers much more than cultivated ones. If I had pots of money, I would keep the paddock ungrazed and have a wild flower meadow.

23rd April – I saw the first butterfly of the year today, a lovely peacock, very large, and heard the first cuckoo. The rabbits are eating the *Anemone japonica* as usual.

Frank and I have now split the herbaceous plants that needed dividing and repositioning. It took only a few hours, but without his help it would have taken me a week. Now that we can see the beds clearly, I notice there are several plants which have succumbed to frost – eight penstemons, two sidalcea and three rue. We usually lose penstemons as they are not fully hardy, but cuttings can be taken in autumn so their loss is not a great problem. I think I can also divide a couple of sidalcea to make up for the lost plants. But the rue bushes will leave large gaps that need to be filled. I will delay replacing them until later in the year to see what comes up and then decide what will go best in these three spots. The beds have changed this year with moving one or two plants and increasing groups of others, so I am not quite sure how everything will look.

We also did one or two other small jobs at odd moments, such as planting summer flowering lilies and galtonia with lots of grit. I split and moved some primulas and potted up several small, self-seeded plants to sell at the garden open day. The budleias have seeded around as usual. They always manage to make quite large plants hidden in the herbaceous foliage over the autumn. They are all about a foot high now. If I needed so many budleias, this would be a very cost-effective plant. But as I do not need any, I hope they will make someone else very happy. The *Tellima grandiflora* is also a good self-seeder. I managed to pot eleven of those.

The weather is continuing changeable. We have had rain, sun, wind and sleet. In 2003 we had a heatwave in April; there was no rain all month. That was the year we laid new turf and then went away for a month! Of course all the turves shrank very badly. I spent two days putting compost in the cracks when I got back.

But usually it snows in April and the daffodils can become battered and bedraggled. The daffodils have been knocked down by the rain a couple of times now, but fortunately this time they quickly sprang up again. I really am determined to plant some more daffodils in the paddock next year, under the large, old, apple tree. I have just been told of somewhere I can buy half a hundredweight of bulbs for £10. At that price it would be a pity not to have a few more. I have also been told that there used to be fields full of small, wild daffodils around here many years ago, before the advent of the mechanical plough. That must have been a magical sight.

28th April – I sowed some seed indoors today and put cowslip seeds in the fridge. According to the seed packet they need to be chilled before they will germinate. The daffodils are finishing now but the larger tulips will be flowering in another week's time.

The lanes and verges are full of anemones, asperula, *Viola odorata*, celandines, wild campanulas and little, white bellflowers now. Everywhere is really very pretty.

The hedgerows around our house are full of wild flowers.

In the garden the young foliage of amelanchiers is a lovely pinky bronze. The elders have their flowers all scrunched up like little cauliflower heads, but the colours are showing, bronze, pink and pale green. The bushes growing over the wall beside the kitchen, *Lonicera pileata*, have tiny, pale green leaves, which are soft to the touch. I brush against them on my way to the washing line. This bush is excellent ground cover, will grow under trees in shade, has very pretty leaves and if planted high up, as mine is, you can see hundreds of delicate, lemony flowers in spring and vibrant, translucent, purple berries in September.

There are many flowers out now, the evergreen wallflower 'Bowles Mauve', primulas, cowslips, polyanthus, blue and white periwinkle, grape hyacinths, chionodoxas, various narcissi, early tulips, viburnums, miniature irises, *Anemone blanda*, aubrietia, a small blue campanula that I do not recognise and euphorbias. They all appeared as if by magic when I was not looking. I have drastically cut down on forget-me-nots this year as they hide a multitude of weeds. It will be easier for us to keep the garden under control for June. The blossom on the fruit trees more

The earliest tulips are always a delight.

180

than makes up for the loss of a few forget-me-nots. The damson, plum and cherry blossom is out now and it will not be long before the apples are in flower. How clever of nature to stagger the effects. One of my favourite shrubs, the amelanchier, is just beginning to have a few starry, white flowers. My niece Rebecca and her young friend Rachel, who are visiting us this weekend for the Ludlow May Fair, wanted to have their photo in this book. The shrub they chose to be photographed with was the amelanchier.

We have lost three-quarters of a huge hypericum by the gas tank and half a cistus by the arbour. How can only half a plant die? If I take these out or cut them back there will be huge gaps, which I will not be able to fill in time for the garden open day. So I have decided to leave them and hope they will simply look like a dark background to brighter flowers.

I thought I had lots of white foxgloves but they have all but

The first blossom appears on the new, young damson, 'Shropshire Prune'.

Chosen above all
others, the
amelanchier.

disappeared. Surely we did not weed them by mistake? This is a huge blow as those stately blocks of white were a highlight of the garden. All I can do is hunt around for seedlings of whatever colour, transplant them and hope for the best. But we have lots of white lupins, so even if the foxglove seedlings are all pink, it will still look beautiful. Another disappointment is the *Verbena bonariensis*. We usually have hundreds of them but I cannot find any. Are they just late to appear? I must find out. A friend thinks they are and will come up eventually, as they flower later in the year and are in no hurry at the moment. They are wonderful in September, light, airy and beautiful and I would have no idea what to replace them with. However, it is always an exciting opportunity when

you lose something, to choose a new plant to put in its place. I know there must be a tall, light and airy annual that will fit the bill, maybe fennel or dill. Despite the losses and the plants we have not found or have not come up yet, the garden looks fresh and pretty. The fields full of lambs around the house are extremely picturesque and the countryside is full of blossom. There is a sense of rebirth and expectation and I would hate to be anywhere else at this time of the year.

How quickly the year has passed for me. This time last year we were arranging Madeline's funeral and could not look ahead further than the next day. This last week of April, Madeline's permanent headstone has just been delivered and we will be putting it beside her parents' memorial in Woburn Sands soon. Life has changed for us again. Now I am looking forward to teaching abroad and holidays later in the year. Tom, my father-in-law, is also moving on. He misses the sea and has decided to move back down to Wales, close to the coast.

But most of all I am looking forward to the garden open day in June, to my friends coming to help and to all those visitors coming to share our enjoyment. Our garden is evolving, it is always full of life and so we are always expecting something new and extraordinary to happen. As usual, I can hardly wait.

Acknowledgements

My husband, Simon, encouraged me to write this little book and my friends Lydia, Linda and Alena pushed me into it! Thank you all.

Jim Price Machinery Ltd (for lawnmowers and servicing)
Farmore Mills
Shrewsbury Road
Craven Arms
Shropshire, SY7 9QG
01588 673746

Botanique Editions
BP 37, Les Beurreries
78810 Feucherolles
France
0033 (0)1 30 54 56 77
www.botaniqueeditions.com

Marshalls Seeds
Alconbury Hill
Huntingdon
Cambridgeshire, PE28 4HY
01480 443390

Jacques Amand
The Nurseries
Clamp Hill
Stanmore
Middlesex, HA7 3JS
0208 420 7110